THE GREAT WAR
AN ILLUSTRATED HISTORY

PHIL CARRADICE

AMBERLEY

About the author:

Phil Carradice is a novelist, poet and historian who has written over forty books. His most recent novel is *The Black Chair* (Gomer), the story of Hedd Wyn, the Welsh poet who was killed at Passchendaele in 1917. He recently produced *Nautical Training Ships* and, with his wife Trudy, *Golf in Wales* for Amberley. He regularly broadcasts on TV and radio and presents *The Past Master*, the BBC Radio Wales history programme.

First published 2010

Amberley Publishing plc
Cirencester Road, Chalford,
Stroud, Gloucestershire, GL6 8PE

www.amberley-books.com

British Library Cataloguing in Publication Data.
A catalogue record for this book is available from the British Library.

ISBN 978 1 84868 881 0

Typeset in 10pt on 13pt Sabon.
Typesetting and Origination by Amberley Publishing.
Printed in the UK.

Contents

Acknowledgements   4

Introduction   5

Causes of the War   8

1914 – The Guns of August   14

1915 – And So It Goes On   43

1916 – The Year of Slaughter   75

1917 – Mud and Blood   98

1918 – The Final Year   131

The Aftermath   147

Notes   157

Bibliography   159

Acknowledgements

Most of the photographs used in this book are from the author's personal collection. However, thanks must go to the following individuals and organisations for allowing the use of certain images:

Roger McCallum
Andrew Swift
The Imperial War Museum

Particular thanks to my grandfather, Robert Turnbull Carradice, for his stories about Egypt, Gallipoli and France. I never thanked you when you were alive, I thank you now. Without your enthusiasm and interest in the subject – talking to me when you would probably have much preferred pottering in your garden – I doubt if this book would ever have been written.

Finally, as ever, thanks to Trudy, my wife.
Your inspiration and determination are legendary.

Introduction

More than any other single event, the Great War of 1914-18 has shaped our view of modern history and our understanding of the world in which we live. Without that terrible, cataclysmic conflict, issues as diverse as votes for women, Irish Home Rule, the creation of Communist Russia and a homeland for Jewish people would no doubt have been delayed and some might never have come to fruition. Certainly the Second World War would never have happened.

The Great War brought to an end dynasties that had ruled over people in Europe for hundreds, perhaps even thousands, of years. The present conflict in Iraq, people have often ventured, is only the latest in a long line of military operations that owe their genesis to the war of 1914-18.

Having said all that, it is a pointless exercise to simply list the consequences or after-effects of the Great War. Such a process would, ultimately, be unfulfilling. Suffice to say that it was one of the most influential events in the history of mankind.

When talking about the war, the writer is immediately faced by the problem of what to call it. The war of 1914-18 was certainly 'great' in so far as it involved almost all the countries of the world, the battles and their effects covering vast swathes of land and sea – and, ultimately, the skies above them as well. It was the first real global conflict, a true 'world war'. Of course, in the years immediately after 1918 this was not called the First World War. Not until 1939-1945 did historians realise that Hitler's war was the second worldwide conflict to erupt within a few short years. Until then everyone simply said 'The war' or used the term Great War. So, for the purposes of this volume, Great War it is.

This book does not purport to be a definitive and detailed history of that first major war of the twentieth century. Such an undertaking would involve far more space than is available here. And besides, it has been done before, many times. Yet, hopefully, the book does have an aim and a specific thrust.

When we think of the war our imaginations and our sensibilities are heavily influenced by the work of a handful of soldier poets, men like Wilfred Owen, Isaac Rosenberg and Siegfried Sassoon. In many respects, our view of the war – lions led by donkeys, needless and mindless sacrifice, men walking helplessly into hails of machine gun fire – is their view. That doesn't mean what they said and wrote was untrue. Quite the opposite, in fact.

But there are other ways and means of looking at the war. This is an illustrated history. The Great War was one of the first conflicts to be readily and effectively covered by artists and photographers and, despite the problems of censorship, at times it seems as if every aspect of the war was caught on camera or by the painter's brush. Therefore, the illustrations are as important here as the text. They catch the mood of the moment, the joy and the horror, the trauma and the delight of defeat and victory.

Death and destruction, the legacy of The Great War. This shows dead German horses in the street of a captured French town, *c.* 1917.

They record the lives of men and women, at the front and at home, on the sea and in the air. They are what make the book different.

This book does not attempt to be the story of the generals and their war. It certainly does not purport to be a blow-by-blow account of the campaigns or the strategy and tactics of the time, although obviously some understanding of the campaigns and what went on is essential. Above all, this is the story of ordinary people caught up in events they could not control and often did not understand. How they coped with the experience, how they lived and died, is what this book is really all about.

At the same time, this is also the story of new inventions, new technology that the war brought into existence or, at least, developed – for good or bad. They were inventions that we have had to live with ever since

Such was the traumatic effect of the Great War that we have now enshrined the pre-war period, the years between the death of Queen Victoria and the guns of 1914, in a golden glow of perfection – the last kick of Edwardian glory, a carefree and happy time when all the world was young. The reality, of course, was very different.

When war was declared in August 1914 it came as something of a distraction for many people. They would never have admitted it but for the upper classes and those in positions of power it brought welcome relief from the stresses and strains of a country and a social class system that were already showing severe signs of strain.

During the Edwardian and early Georgian periods there was real poverty and disease, not to mention death and disorder, in many of Britain's cities where the vision of writers like Dickens and Arthur Morrison had not yet vanished under the application of a welfare state.

Civil unrest marked several of the years leading up to 1914, the generals of the British Army seeming to be as happy to turn the guns of their soldiers against striking workers as they were against the Boers and Zulus of South Africa. Ireland seemed on the point of open rebellion and there was a real possibility of civil war in what was, really, Britain's oldest colony.

Above left: Kaiser Wilhelm II of Germany was a great target for political cartoonists throughout the war.

Above right: German prisoners are marched to the quayside, ready for transportation to England and incarceration in a prisoner-of-war camp, *c.* 1915.

The growth of the Labour Party, the idea that working men and women might have minds of their own, and the demand for universal suffrage were, for many of the upper classes, the thin end of the wedge.

For the ordinary working man in the street the war spelled adventure. In those days most people were born, lived and died in the same town or village and geographical mobility was largely unknown. So the possibility of travel to foreign places, of taking part in a jaunt with mates from the farm or factory, was hugely appealing. It meant, for a while at least, the end of a humdrum and boring existence.

At least, that was how it began. Over the next four years the men who volunteered so gladly – and those who continued to enlist, either as volunteers or, after 1916, as conscripts – found themselves embroiled in an experience that shaped and shattered their lives. It was such a profound shock that many of them never stopped talking about it for the rest of their days. For some, they retreated into a shell, behind a wall of silence that could never be breached.

Not in 1914. Then it was all a game, a joke that everyone could understand and appreciate. It was a time when the phrase 'It'll all be over by Christmas' had real significance. It was not just a saying to be glibly banded about but a real and actual threat – the thought of the war ending before the volunteers of 1914 reached the front line was something not to be considered in too much detail. Nobody wanted to be left out.

It was little wonder, then, that the first few months of the war brought a huge influx of men to the colours. They came in their thousands, all eager to 'do their bit' and get to the front while there was still time to get a swipe at the Hun! God bless the King and Empire, all praise to Harry and St George, they thought – even if they could not easily express their emotions or the sentiment. If only they knew how wrong they were!

Causes of the War

As well as being hugely complex, the causes of the Great War are many and varied. In some respects the conflict came about when the game of international brinkmanship that had been raging for years, in greater or lesser degrees, finally reached a point where a bluff was called and nobody was prepared to back down. The assassination in Sarajevo might have been the match that ignited the powder keg but the fuse had been lit and was simmering for many years before that event.

During the second half of the nineteenth century, the five great nations of Europe – Germany, France, Britain, Austria-Hungary and Russia – had built themselves into vast power blocks. These were power blocks that appeared impregnable but which, when carefully analysed, can be seen to have been built on foundations of sand.

Germany, the newest industrial and military power in Europe, was eager to establish herself 'a place in the sun'. The country, as an entity, had not existed before 1870 when Otto von Bismarck forged a united Germany out of several disparate states, under the ambitious and militaristic leadership of Prussia. Victory in the Franco-Prussian War of 1870 merely confirmed the power of this new, dynamic and embryonic state in the heart of Europe.

As the twentieth century unfolded, industrialists in Germany were clear that they did not want war with any of the other great nations; they knew that economic strength alone would soon elevate the country to the forefront of European powers. Militarily, however, it was a different matter. By the summer of 1914 the German Army, building on the successes of the Franco-Prussian War, stood supreme, the most powerful fighting force in the world. Knowing that the key to the country's economic and colonial success was her navy, Germany was also engaged in a dramatic arms race with Britain, building dreadnought battleships and cruisers at a phenomenal rate, in order to challenge the Royal Navy.

Yet things were not quite as clear cut as they first appeared. The armies of France and Russia were also developing and growing. Within a few years they would undoubtedly match the strength of Germany. And for every dreadnought built by Germany, Britain was building an equivalent – and more. Germany might wish for colonies and an Empire but Britain was certainly not prepared to stand aside and allow her position as the premier trading country in the world to be taken over by a rapaciously hungry Germany.

Because of these factors, there is a school of thought that says August 1914 was the ideal moment for Germany to start a war. And yet, in that last glorious summer, it seemed as if the great powers were closer in understanding and viewpoint than they had ever been.

The potential crisis over Germany's desire to build a railway from Berlin to Baghdad, a problem that had been simmering since 1899, seemed to have been resolved. Kaiser Wilhelm of Germany, King George V of Britain and Czar Nicholas of Russia were cousins who, right to the end, maintained friendly relations with each other. In France, a socialist government had recently been returned and the French were rapidly moving

Emblem here of rage—amaze—
Poor deluded caddie says:
" Hello, Bill, we're bunkered."

The cartoonist strikes again. The Kaiser, with a hapless Austrian soldier as his caddy, finds himself bunkered and without any way out when confronted with the combined might of the Allies.

Above left: Kaiser Wilhelm II of Germany in a suitably martial pose. He became Kaiser in June 1888; the grandson of Queen Victoria, at one time he was sixth in line to the British throne. A difficult breech birth left him with a withered left arm, something he strove to conceal in most portraits, like this one.

Above right: Czar Nicholas II of Russia succeeded to the throne in 1894. A weak and ineffective ruler, he was by temperament a mild mannered man but Russian politics demanded he rule as a despot. Defeat for Russia in the Russo-Japanese War led to the first Revolution in 1905. This in turn led Nicholas to reopen the Duma, a Parliament for the people – it was, for his regime, the thin end of the wedge.

to a position of tentative friendship with Germany. That was how it seemed, on the surface at least – yet again it paid to look deeper as this was a false picture, a veneer that covered far too many cracks.

Suspicion and obligation were major factors in the build up to war. All of the great powers were naturally suspicious of each other, afraid that alliances would be formed between enemies or rivals, leaving them alone and isolated. There was no mechanism in existence at that time to settle or arbitrate in disputes and in many quarters war was regarded as a natural consequence, even as a welcome process that might renew and refresh a nation's blood stock.

And so, because they saw no other way, in the early years of the twentieth century the great powers began to form alliances with each other, alliances that, once war began, would start to tumble together and fall like a stack of dominoes.

Germany and Austria-Hungary, as natural allies, soon signed a mutual defence alliance, each promising to help if the other country should ever be attacked. In 1901, France and Russia did likewise, the Czar promising that, in the event of war between Germany and France, Russia would launch an attack on Germany within eighteen days. Britain, bolstered and protected by its navy, maintained an aloof stance from the countries of mainland Europe. However, she did deign to reach a diplomatic and military understanding with France, her traditional enemy. In 1907, she came to a similar arrangement with Russia, thus creating the Entente Cordiale.

These alliances seemed to determine the safety of each individual country and guarantee the peace of Europe. In reality they were rigid stockades that did little more than ensure that if one great power went to war with another, the rest of Europe would be quickly dragged in.

A superb political postcard from the early years of the Great War, showing the extent of German influence across central Europe.

Assassination

The immediate cause of war was the assassination of Archduke Franz Ferdinand in Sarajevo on 28 June 1914.

For some time the rulers of Austria-Hungary had believed that the stability and security of her Empire in the Balkans was under threat from Serbia. The Balkan provinces of Bosnia and Herzegovina had been relatively recent acquisitions from Turkey, coming under the administration of Austria-Hungary in the years immediately after 1878. They were only finally annexed by the Hapsburg dynasty in 1908. The Austro-Hungarian Empire in these Balkan provinces contained over 20,000,000 Serbs, Slavs and Croats and, with Serbia increasingly seeing herself as the leader of a Pan Slav movement, there was considerable resentment in these people, particularly among the young, that they had been made part of the Austro-Hungarian Empire rather than being allowed to join Serbia.

It became almost a national pastime for students to gather together in the cafés or book shops of cities like Sarajevo and plan how they might change things. Wanting independence, wanting to break away from foreign rule, was nothing new – what was new was the willingness of these students to use violence to achieve their aims. And so, when it was announced that Archduke Franz Ferdinand, heir to the Hapsburg monarchy, would come to inspect the Austrian Army in Bosnia in the early summer of 1914, a group of young Serbs decided they would try to assassinate him.

The students received encouragement and were given weapons – revolvers, bombs and cyanide with which to kill themselves rather than be captured – by a Serbian secret society called The Black Hand. The links between The Black Hand, led by the mysterious Colonel Dragutin Dimitrijevic or Colonel Apis as he was invariably known, and the Serbian government remain unclear but over the next few weeks the students carefully laid their plans. [1]

The Archduke had decided to bring his wife Sophie with him to Bosnia. Sophie was not of royal blood; theirs was a morganatic marriage, their children barred from the succession. The only time she could even sit beside him, in state, was when he was

Emperor Franz Joseph of Austria, an old and implacably conservative Emperor who guided Austria-Hungary into the war after his nephew was killed in Sarajevo. Franz Joseph died in 1916, being succeeded by Charles, the last Emperor of Austria-Hungary.

Erzherzog Thronfolger Franz Ferdinand ... und Gemahlin Herzogin Sophie von ...

Left: The Archduke Franz Ferdinand, heir to the throne of Austria-Hungary, and his wife Sophie, together for once in public. Not of his rank, she was relegated to a secondary position whenever there were public duties to perform.

Below: Moments before the fatal shooting on the morning of 28 June 1914, the Archduke's car begins to turn down Franz Joseph Street. Gavrilo Princip was waiting under the trees on the left of the photograph and could not believe his luck when the official car drew up in front of him.

engaged in his duties as Inspector General of the Austro-Hungarian forces. And the visit to Bosnia was just such an occasion. Sophie would, he decided, enjoy a spectacular day out. Franz Ferdinand and his wife duly arrived in Sarajevo on the morning of 28 June, driving straight into the arms of the waiting conspirators. At first, however, things did not go quite the way the students had planned.

At least one student decided not to go ahead with the murder and returned home before the Archduke appeared. Another would-be assassin, Nedjo Cabrinovic, hurled a bomb at the royal car as it passed his position. The bomb hit the hood of the car – folded down for comfort in the hot weather – bounced into the road and exploded in front of the car following behind. Several of the conspirators, hearing the bang of the explosion, either ducked down or failed to intervene and the Archduke's car drove on to a reception at the town hall. Franz Ferdinand was furious – his wife's great day out had been thoroughly spoiled.

Due to the assassination attempt the route of the Archduke's return journey was now changed. Rather than turn right into Franz Joseph Street – a route that would have taken the royal party through the narrow alleys and streets of the city centre – it was decided to take the fast way out of town, down the long straight road known as Appel Quay. Unfortunately, nobody thought of telling the drivers.

The leading car in the column slowed and turned into Franz Joseph Street. The Archduke's vehicle began to follow. Then, realising the mistake, the drivers stopped their cars and prepared to reverse. But the mistake had brought Franz Ferdinand under the gaze of a short dark man with hollow eyes, a man holding a Browning pistol in his right hand. This was Gavrilo Princip, the most fanatical and dedicated of all the would-be assassins.

Princip took aim and fired, once, twice. At first it seemed as if the shots had missed their mark. Both the Archduke and his wife sat, peaceful and still, in their seats, but as the car began to move once more the Duchess fell forward, over the lap of her husband. And then the aides and dignitaries in the car with the royal couple saw blood begin to spurt from the mouth of Franz Ferdinand.

The Archduke collapsed back onto the seat muttering 'It's nothing, nothing.' Then, glancing down at his wife, he whispered 'Sophie, live for the children.' They were his last words. The car was driven rapidly to a nearby hospital, doctors running alongside the vehicle as it went. It was no use. Franz Ferdinand had been hit by a single shot, the bullet lodging in his spine, and he breathed his last shortly after reaching the hospital. Sophie had died a few minutes earlier. [2]

In the wake of the shooting Gavrilo Princip tried, first, to turn his gun on himself. It was wrestled off him and he was seized and beaten by the crowd. Saved by the local police and military, he tried to swallow the cyanide he had been given by The Black Hand. It did not work and simply made him sick.

Princip was later tried and imprisoned, dying of tuberculosis of the bones in 1918. His death, coming as it did in the wake of 10,000,000 others, went largely unnoticed. But he had done his work in July 1914.

1914 – The Guns of August

Mobilisation

The Austro-Hungarian government was adamant that they knew where the blame lay for the assassination of Franz Ferdinand. Backed by their German allies, they decided it was time to take a hard line with Serbia. Despite the fact that no proof was ever found to implicate the Serbian government, on 25 July 1914 an ultimatum was presented to Serbia. It was an ultimatum that effectively laid all blame and responsibility for the killings on the Serbs and, more importantly, put the country under the thrall of Austria-Hungary.

The ultimatum was designed to humiliate and subjugate the people Austria felt had organised the assassination. Among other things it required Serbia to suppress all anti-Austrian societies and remove from the army anyone who was suspected of anti-Austrian sympathies. Nobody expected Serbia to accept such harsh terms but, desperate to avoid further bloodshed, the Serbian government agreed to eight out of the ten demands. The two that had been rejected were so minor that nobody even considered them worth bothering with.

The mood in Vienna, however, was belligerent. The heir to the Hapsburg monarchy had been killed and many Austrians felt that something had to be done to put the Serbs in their place. The reply was not good enough and three days after the Serbian answer was received Austria-Hungary formally declared war on Serbia. Even now, disaster could have been averted as the Austrian Army still had to mobilise and clearly would not have been ready for several weeks but nobody had either the skill or the inclination to step in and mediate.

Russia, as a predominantly Slav state, had long felt under an obligation to support Serbia in any conflict – and, of course, a German/Austro-Hungarian dominance in the Balkans, effectively blocking and controlling the way to Constantinople, could not be tolerated by the Russian government. On 30 July 1914, Russia mobilised her forces. The Russians did not want war – this was merely a game of brinkmanship, an answer to Austria-Hungary's aggressive posturing.

Russia, like most of the great powers, had a huge standing army, over one million men, plus a vast reserve of conscript soldiers. To mobilise these forces involved an immense logistical exercise, relying mainly on railway trains and, of course, on railway timetables. And once railway trains and wagons began to roll they had to continue moving, otherwise there would be an enormous log jam of men and machinery. Communication was not easy in 1914 and trying to halt or change the destination of several thousand soldiers was a complex process.

Mobilisation was a dilemma that also faced Germany. If the Germans did not mobilise against Russia in support of their allies and act speedily, they would be forced

Kaiser Wilhelm was a troubled, unhappy soul with a deep envy of Britain and her place in the world. Despite his damaged left arm he was a great supporter of the military and built up Germany's army and navy in order to challenge the other nations of Europe. This photograph shows him in the first year of the war, waiting to welcome the Emperor of Austria.

to fight a war on two fronts as France, already joined by treaty to Russia, had indicated that she would abide by the terms of their agreement.

As a consequence, Germany sent an ultimatum to Russia, demanding that she demobilise her forces. The demand was refused and, on 1 August, Germany declared war on Russia. Two days later, in an attempt to pre-empt the French, war was also declared on France. Almost without realising it, without even wanting it, the great powers of Europe had slid into a war.

Britain remained, imperious and alone, on the sidelines. It was not to last long. Germany had been only too aware that she might, one day, have to fight a war on two fronts, against Russia and France at the same time. Consequently, Count von Schlieffen, Chief of the German General Staff between 1891 and 1907, had come up with an ingenious and totally unscrupulous plan of campaign. The frontier between Germany and France was short and heavily defended but to the north lay the relatively open plains of Belgium.

Although notionally a neutral country, a lightning strike through Belgium, followed by an encircling and outflanking right hook to the south and east, should, von Schlieffen reasoned, knock France out of any war in a matter of just six weeks. It was a desperate stroke but, in light of the alliances and power blocks between the nations, in 1914 it was the only plan that Germany possessed.

The plan had been drawn up long before 1914 and von Schlieffen had been dead for almost half a dozen years when, on 2 August, Germany demanded free passage for her armies through Belgium. Understandably enough, the Belgians refused and, when German troops rolled regardless into the country on 4 August, Britain found herself on the edge of conflict.

In a treaty signed seventy-four years earlier, in 1830, Britain had guaranteed Belgium's territorial safety, a treaty so ancient that many people thought it had lapsed. It hadn't and Britain had little alternative but to stand by her obligations. A British ultimatum for German forces to leave Belgian territory expired, unanswered, at midnight on 4 August and, almost before people knew what was happening, Britain found herself at war with Germany.

Parademarsch im Regiment (Schluss des Regiments).

Mobilisation of troops effectively meant war as there was no way to stop the machinery once it had been set in motion. This shows German soldiers, complete with pickelhaub helmets, marching off to the front in 1914.

British Reservists and Territorials were also being mobilised in the early days of August. And then there were the volunteers, thousands of eager young men who rushed forward to answer Lord Kitchener's call for 100,000 more troops.

As the Schlieffen Plan demanded, the German attack was through Belgium. This shows German troops marching in the hot August sunshine. Now, you will notice, their pickelhaubs are covered by canvas.

Britain at War

4 August 1914 – a Bank Holiday in Britain, one of the few statutory days off enjoyed by working class people – had been a day of stupendous heat. Seizing the chance for an enjoyable day out, many people took a charabanc or railway trip to the seaside. When they returned from their excursions to Brighton or Margate or Southend later that night they learned, to their amazement, that the country was about to go to war with Germany. The news was greeted, not with shock or horror but by an outpouring of excitement and unbridled joy.

This moment was, for many, a high tide of jingoism. Crowds thronged the Mall, singing, dancing and screaming for the King to show himself on the balcony of Buckingham Palace. The Kaiser, the man who had dared to challenge the might of the Royal Navy, was at last about to receive a well-deserved 'bloody nose'. But for those in the know, for those with a deeper understanding of the ramifications of war, there were many reservations.

It is recorded that on the eve of the war Sir Edward Grey, British Foreign Secretary, stood at his window and watched a lamplighter at work in the street outside. 'The lights are going out all over Europe,' he supposedly remarked. 'I do not think we shall see them lit again in our time.' Whether or not Grey actually uttered those words is a matter of conjecture but they certainly catch the mood of the moment.

Reservists were immediately called up, along with Territorials, part-time soldiers who, initially at least, were intended to serve only in Britain. They went, in the main, in total ignorance. The last conflict between the major powers had been the Franco-Prussian War of 1870 and Britain had not been involved. The Boer War had finished a dozen years before and that, apart from sieges of places like Mafeking and Ladysmith, was a war of movement, fought mainly by cavalry units. Nobody in 1914 had the slightest idea of what was waiting for them. [3]

Britain had always depended on the Royal Navy for the defence of her shores and, consequently, the British Army stood at just 250,000 men – a mere handful when compared to the 800,000 of Germany and the million plus available to Russia – used simply to quell native revolts and take part in the odd colonial skirmish. In August 1914, many of these troops were still serving in distant parts of the Empire – it would be months before they could be recalled. However, treaty obligations meant that Britain was now committed to sending an expeditionary force to fight in France and Belgium. Clearly, in the months ahead, Britain would require a volunteer army of some size and substance.

Within days of the declaration of war, the British Expeditionary Force was quickly assembled, some 90,000 men in one cavalry and four infantry divisions. Under the command of Sir John French they marched to the south coast and by 8 August were beginning to take ship for France. They came ashore, in the main, at Le Havre and moved to a concentration area by train and, in some cases, by London buses that had been hastily pressed into service. By 13 August they had taken up position on the left flank of the French Army and had begun to move forward into Belgium. [4]

Above left: The British flocked to enlist, convinced the war would be over by Christmas. No stone was left unturned when it came to appealing for men – postcards like this were on sale all over the country.

Above right: Sir Edward Grey, Secretary of State for Foreign Affairs, a man at the heart of the crisis.

Within a week of the declaration of war the British Expeditionary Force had been assembled and was beginning to take ship for France. This photograph shows British infantry arriving in France, all eager to give the Kaiser 'a bloody nose'.

The First Shots

Adhering to the broad remit of the Schlieffen Plan, the German High Command also acted swiftly. Between 4 and 6 August over 500 railway trains thundered across the Rhine bridges as German forces, under Generals von Kluck and von Bulow, poured like armies of ants into Belgium. Somebody once calculated that the war which began on that day was in fact the 980th war in the history of mankind. Whether or not that calculation is correct, the war that was just beginning was to be long and terrible and nobody had ever seen its like before.

The border towns of Namur and Liege were besieged and quickly taken by the advancing Germans, the fortresses being battered to pieces by heavy artillery shells. But the Belgians would not go down without a fight. They pulled back to Antwerp, destroying railway lines, engines and rolling stock behind them as they went. This scorched earth policy caused major disruption to the German Army, slowing but not stopping the advance.

Belgian civilians fled, possessions piled onto carts, all desperate to get away before the Germans arrived. Like lemmings they stretched out along the cobbled roads, blocking the way for military traffic, none of them really knowing where they were headed or what would become of them.

Inevitably, there were tales of atrocities committed by the 'barbaric' German invaders, stories that would, in the weeks and months ahead, be embellished many times. Atrocities did take place and the Germans were undoubtedly harsh in their treatment of some villages and towns. But the stories of burning babies and the massacre of nuns that were commonplace in the British press were gross exaggerations with one purpose – to put the whole country behind the war effort.

Meanwhile, the French, under their charismatic General Joseph 'Pappa' Joffre, decided that attack was the best form of defence and, in the wooded Ardennes region, the French Army cut into the wheeling left flank of the encircling Germans. It was an uneven contest. Clad in their traditional blue and red uniforms, the French were mown down in their thousands and the attacks quickly ground to a halt. In support, the British Expeditionary Force (the BEF) advanced steadily and carefully towards the

Faced by superior German forces the Belgian Army had no choice but to pull back and surrender large parts of their country to the invader. But as they went they carried out a scorched earth policy, destroying railway trains and other means of transport behind them – as this shows.

The Allied press quickly seized on stories of German barbarity. In the absence of photographic evidence, cartoonists and artists produced their own versions of the horrors – and were believed implicitly.

The fear of spies and Fifth Columnists was everywhere. Even refugees, fleeing from the German advance, were subjected to searches.

The Battle of Mons was the first contact between British and German forces. The British Army might have been small but it was very efficient and the quality of their rifle fire took the Germans by surprise.

One of several last ditch stands by British forces at Mons and during the subsequent retreat. This shows the final stand of the guns of L. Battery, Royal Horse Artillery. The sacrifice of units such as these enabled the BEF to withdraw in good order.

THE ROYAL ARTILLERY.
The Last Stand of L Battery at Mons.

The retreat from Mons was a crippling and dangerous withdrawal in intense heat, made all the more galling for the British since they had advanced up the same roads only a few days before.

Belgian Field Artillery in a relaxed moment before the next German onslaught.

Sambre River and the line of the Mons-Conde Canal. Another French attack in the south, in the Alsace Loraine area – French territory that had been ceded to Germany after the Franco-Prussian War – was also repelled at this time.

The first contact between British and German forces came at Mons on 23 August, when two British Divisions were attacked by considerably larger German forces. So accurate was the British rifle fire – supposedly fifteen rounds rapid in a minute – that the Germans thought they were being fired on by machine guns. In the face of such a fusillade, the German advance ground to a halt.

The legend of the Angels of Mons dates from this time, one of several fanciful tales that were dutifully reported in the national press. The legend states that British troops were aided by a band of angels that fought beside them at Mons – a morale boosting story that owes far more to the imaginative pen of Welsh journalist Arthur Machen than it ever does to reality. Another popular story from these weeks was of Russian soldiers seen marching through France or Scotland – the location varies – with snow on their boots. In reality these 'Russians' were probably members of a Scottish regiment, wearing white spats and talking in a broad Highland brogue that would have been unintelligible to most people.

Following the clash at Mons, Sir John French had intended to fight again the following day. Then he was informed that the French were withdrawing, moving back to defend Paris. Realising that the BEF was now totally isolated, Sir John had no option but to order a similar withdrawal. It was a hard fighting retreat through boiling heat, pursued by a dogged and determined enemy. Several times the BEF was in danger of being completely cut off, only last-ditch stands by individual units of infantry and artillery saving the day.

On 26 August, Sir John French decided to turn and fight once more. At the Battle of Le Cateau the Germans were halted yet again. It was a brutal and hard-fought slugging match but it gave the British – and their disorganised allies – a breathing space of almost ten days.

If the effect of the fighting retreat on the British had been dramatic, the advancing Germans felt the strain almost as much. One of the disadvantages of the Schlieffen Plan was that those soldiers marching on the outside of the arc, the part closest to the Belgian coast, had to travel faster and further than those on the inside of the circle. And they weren't just marching; they were fighting too, hard grinding battles like Mons and Le Cateau. Within a few weeks they were, quite simply, exhausted and the German advance simply ran out of steam. It was, however, only a temporary respite.

Selling the War

While the members of the British Expeditionary Force were fighting and dying in the fields and ditches of Belgium and northern France, events back home in Britain had been proceeding apace.

It was a time for heroes. As early as 6 August, Field Marshal Kitchener, the victor of the Sudan and the South African campaign, then on leave from his position as Governor of Egypt, had been appointed Secretary of State for War. With everyone predicting that the war would be over by Christmas – even the Kaiser commented that his troops would be back in Germany 'before the leaves fall from the trees' – Kitchener shocked the establishment by declaring that it would last for at least three years. More importantly, he said, Britain must plan for exactly that eventuality.

Kitchener proposed that an army of 100,000 volunteers should be immediately raised. And to help in creating this new volunteer army, recruiting posters, backed up by rallies and recruiting events, were suddenly in evidence all over the country. In the music halls and theatres professional singers and actresses sang 'We don't want to lose you/But we think you ought to go' and Lord Kitchener's moustachioed face seemed to stare out from every hoarding. 'Remember brave little Belgium' was the cry and men flocked to the colours in their thousands. They were not soldiers and training them for the task would take time. But the required volunteer army had begun its life and was steadily growing.

Kitchener's target, the first hundred thousand men, was easily reached and then superseded many times. It seemed as if every able bodied man in the country was either in the army or about to join up. This was the time of 'the white feather', tokens of cowardice that were presented to any man not in uniform or suspected of malingering, while papers like *The Penarth Times* in South Wales were more than happy to lend weight to the recruiting campaign. Like many other local and regional papers, *The Penarth Times* published a leader article commenting that:

> 'Our young men go about in their tennis rig-outs or parade on the Esplanade, smirking at girls. Is it fair that they should go about so callously whilst those who took up arms with our promised support, lie cold and stiff. Give the laggards their marching orders, shame them into understanding where their duty lies.' 5

There had, initially, been some opposition to the war from the churches and chapels. It was a European conflict, they declared; why not leave the fighting to the French and Germans? But as news of the German atrocities in Belgium – greatly exaggerated by the popular press – became common knowledge, a huge groundswell of public opinion began to gather behind the war effort.

Lord Kitchener was the most famous soldier in Britain. He had commanded the relieving force at Khartoum and had effectively won the Boer War for the Empire.

Visé Paris n° 109
GUERRE 1914-1915. — Infanterie anglaise en embuscade. — Infantry laring cower. — LL.

This shows British infantry heading for cover in the days when the war was still a war of movement.

Above left: The most famous recruiting poster of the war, Lord Kitchener appeals directly to the British public. Within days of the poster appearing on the walls, fences and hoardings of British cities his projected 100,000 men had been surpassed, many times.

Above right: Remember gallant little Belgium was the cry of many in the early days of the war. It was a fallacy – this was a war to protect not a small country in danger, but Britain's position as a world leader. It was a war to keep Germany in her place. But it was far better to appeal to the fair play of the British and to show care for the underdog.

Patriotic postcards began to appear in huge numbers. Many of them took the Kaiser firmly to task and the cartoons of Louis Raemaekers, condemning Germany for her actions, were much in demand. So powerful were Raemaekers' drawings that the German government even put a price on his head. Raemaekers' drawings were imitated by other artists, of lesser and greater talent but here, in the early months of the war, the idea of the Official War Artist was spawned.

In the local and national newspapers, poems – sometimes, in the days before censorship, actually written by soldiers serving in France or Belgium – were regularly printed. They may not have been great poetry but in an emotional time when even someone like Siegfried Sassoon was writing 'We are the happy legion, for we know/ Time's but a golden wind that shakes the grass' they summed up the mood of the nation. So soldiers were happy to write lines such as these:

> May God defend our country
> Is the cry of everyone;
> This war is forced upon us,
> Welcomed by none.
> But when the conflict's over,
> Some in a hero's grave,
> Heroic deeds shall then be told
> Of Britain's brave.
> (C. Allen) [6]

There was not much doubt among soldiers of all nations that God was on their side. And, equally as important, everyone felt that they were fighting not a war of aggression, but a conflict that had been forced on them. As such it was a war of defence. One German soldier was moved to write the following:

> You only wanted peace, you swore –
> And secretly prepared for war:
> O Nicolas, O Nicolas, you are a lying bugger.
>
> O Engeland, O Engeland, how badly you've behaved,
> Just like a common bloody thief
> Who fancies all the world's his fief:
> O Engeland, O Engeland, this time you'll not be saved.
> (Wilhem Platz) [7]

Sometimes the poems were much more specific, taking battles or skirmishes and using them as the topic and theme of the poem:

> In a dirty ditch I'm lying, midst
> The dying and the dead
> With a piece of shrapnel sticking in
> My dazed and aching head.

The German advance through Belgium was fast and furious. But it was not without cost. This shows a dead German soldier outside Antwerp, a curious sight for adults and children alike.

For I've been sorely stricken in
The carnage that befell
Among the Seaforth Highlanders
That day at Neuve Chapel.
(A. T. Rixon) [8]

The wonder is not that soldier poets, most of them with limited educational levels or standards, could write such verses but that the papers, many of them with circulations in the tens of thousands, should actually publish them. Clearly it was regarded as good for public morale.

The Battle of the Marne

In northern France and Belgium, after a ten day respite, the German juggernaut began to roll again. Now, however, rather than continue with the wide encircling movement called for by the Schlieffen Plan, von Kluck's First Army swung to the left, eastwards of Paris, where he felt there were better lines of communication with the forces of his compatriot Prince von Bulow. The German Commander-in-Chief, General von Moltke, far away from the point of conflict, agreed with this decision.

This drastic change of direction utterly destroyed von Schlieffen's carefully worked out strategy. But initially, at least, it seemed to be the right move. By 5 September German troops had crossed the River Marne and here they were immediately harried by the armies of Gallieni, the military governor of Paris, and by those of 'Pappa' Joffre. Despite the desperate French attacks, the Germans moved inexorably onwards, some units of their army eventually finding themselves within fifteen miles of the French capital. Once more the roads were crowded with refugees but this time the terrified men and women pushing the carts and wagons were French, many of them from Paris itself.

On 7 September, with French and German forces desperately battling for supremacy, General Gallieni created one of the great legends of the war when he ordered every taxi cab in Paris to be commandeered by the military. Filled with replacements and

Selfridge's Department Store in London was one of several central locations where the latest news was posted for all to see – before it appeared in next day's newspapers.

SELFRIDGE'S "War Window" In this window were displayed maps, bulletins, etc., of the Balkan War. It is now being used for the same purpose during the present great War.

German prisoners being led away to captivity, c. 1915.

98   GUERRE DE 1914. — Officiers Allemands prisonniers   LL.
Reproduction interdite

Army transport was limited in the early days of the war and all types of vehicle were commandeered. This shows old London buses in use to take men up to the front lines.

reserves, these taxis then took the soldiers forty miles to the front, several of them making five or six journeys each. The story of the Paris taxi cabs and their part in the eventual victory on the Marne has gone down in French folklore.

Faced by furious assaults from Gallieni on his flank, von Kluck withdrew his leading troops in order to deal with these French attacks. It opened a thirty mile wide gap between the two German armies and into this Joffre insisted that John French must thrust the BEF. To the amazement of Sir John he found virtually no opposition even though his allies were fighting desperately on either side of him.

At this crucial moment, as in so much of the war, British leadership promptly failed. Sir John French seemed incapable of operating independently or of using his initiative. His advance was too slow and failed to exploit the gap, even though, on occasions, his leading cavalry detachments were twenty or thirty miles behind the German front line.

Despite this clear failure in leadership, the appearance of British troops was disheartening for the Germans and von Moltke felt he had no alternative but to order a withdrawal. Soon the tactical withdrawal became a full-scale retreat. It was a distressing and depressing moment for the German troops – they had, after all, been within touching distance of their objective. The Battle of the Marne had been won by the French and, virtually without firing a shot, by a strangely hesitant and reluctant British Expeditionary Force.

The Race to the Sea

The German retreat lasted for just over five days. They fell back on all flanks, searching for the most suitable spot to stabilise their line. They found it along the River Aisne where they were at last able to scratch out some simple and basic holes in the earth and set up defensive positions. They expected to be immediately attacked and overrun but, by now, both sides were utterly exhausted. The BEF managed to cross the Aisne and fight the largely ineffective and totally unnecessary Battle of the Aisne, but then the Allies simply slowed their advance and stopped.

Both sides now 'dug in', creating trenches to protect themselves and to mount what was already becoming one of the most significant weapons of the war, the hugely destructive machine gun. Sir John French, proving himself a more effective prophet than general, remarked:

> 'I think the battle of the Aisne is very typical of what battles in the future are most likely to resemble ... the spade will be as great a necessity as the rifle.'

As it stood, the flanks of both the Germans and the Allies remained wide open, particularly in the north, between the Aisne and the sea. In a desperate attempt to get around or turn the others flank there now began what is known as the 'race to the sea' – even though neither side was actually tying to reach the coast, they were simply attempting to get around the others flank.

The BEF swept towards St Omer and Ypres. Both towns were strategically significant, St Omer blocking the way to Boulogne, Ypres the way to Calais. The Channel ports were important for the British as not only were they docks through which reinforcements

Bicycles were another way of getting to the front line and of moving men around from one position to the next. They were also used by scouts, trying to fix enemy positions.

and supplies could be funnelled, they were also places that, should they be needed, could act as bases for evacuation.

Extending the lines northwards, both sides looked for features that would be important in any future battle. In general, the Germans managed to find whatever high ground was available – it wasn't much. The British line ran reasonably straight but at Ypres it bulged out into German territory, creating a salient that as the war progressed would become the site of the greatest prolonged bloodbath Europe had ever seen.

The First Battle of Ypres took place in October 1914, during the race to the sea as each side tried to outflank the other. The Germans advanced on Ypres at exactly the same moment as the British came up from the south and the two forces, almost literally, ran into each other.

Outnumbered and badly led by Sir John French and his Divisional commanders, the British troops put up a heroic struggle but, at one stage, the German advance troops smashed right through the centre of the British line. They were faced only by cooks and clerks but reinforcements were rushed to the spot and the crisis passed.

In the end the Battle of Ypres petered out, the town and salient remaining in British hands. But victory, if victory it was, did not come before the old regular British Army – the Old Contemptibles as they were labelled, not by the Kaiser as was popularly believed but by the British government itself – was virtually destroyed as a fighting force.

British casualties numbered some 50,000, a mere handful when compared to the German losses of 150,000, but these were the cream of British soldiery, the backbone of the small but highly professional British Army. These were the men who, for years, had served throughout the Empire, on the North West Frontier and in the Burmese jungles. They had fought, bravely and magnificently, at Mons and Le Cateau. Now, largely, they were gone and the handful that was left was soon to perish at battles such as Neuve Chapelle and Loos.

In the future their places would be taken by the Territorials and the vast conscript and volunteer armies that were, even now, beginning to build and grow back home in

A convoy of British
soldiers crossing a
river by a hastily
erected pontoon
bridge.

The cost of war. This
shows a munitions
convoy caught in
the open by German
artillery.

The digging of
trenches soon became
crucial in a war
where movement
was severely limited.
The men here have
time and space to dig
their trenches, which
presupposes it was a
practise exercise in the
rear areas. Normally,
digging trenches was
done under the gaze of
the enemy and often
while under fire
as well.

Barbed wire was an essential element of any trench system, miles of the stuff being laid down on both sides of the lines. Many men, during an attack or even a raid, found themselves caught on the wire and therefore totally vulnerable to enemy fire.

Searching for the grave of a fallen comrade.

The trenches were wet, cold and unhealthy. Pumping out the water that gathered at the trench bottom was a daily chore.

Above left: British artillery assembling a field gun.

Above right: From the beginning, Germany realised that her greatest enemy was not the French – even though they had more men fighting – but the British. This German postcard shows the significance of the island nation to the Germans.

Britain. But it would take time for these replacements to arrive, let alone become an effective fighting force.

For the time being the French would have to shoulder the main burden as far as fighting was concerned. And they knew it. Britain and France had, traditionally, been enemies for hundreds of years. Only relatively recently had there been any accord or agreement between them and much mutual animosity remained. It was from this period in time that the famous French saying arose – Britain would happily fight to the last Frenchman.

Despite Winston Churchill, First Lord of the Admiralty, sending 3,000 troops of the Naval Division (among them the poet Rupert Brooke) to aid in its defence, Antwerp fell to the Germans on 10 October and by the twentieth of the month the line of trenches was stabilised and well established. There were to be minor movements and alterations over the next four years but, generally speaking, the line of trenches, reaching over four hundred miles from the Swiss border to the Belgian coast, remained virtually unchanged until the Germans pulled back to newly prepared positions in 1917.

The War in the East

As the German advance in the west stuttered to a halt, the situation in the east did not seem much better. Despite everyone's predictions, the Russians had managed to mobilise quite speedily and, by the middle of August, two huge armies under Generals Samsonov and Rennenkampf were already pushing towards German territory.

Early clashes led to Russian victories and the German commander, von Prittwitz, actually considered that retreat was his only option. When he heard the news, von Moltke immediately sacked von Prittwitz and appointed the sixty-eight-year-old

Paul von Hindenburg in his place. Hindenburg brought with him as his Chief of Staff a soldier who had recently achieved considerable success in Belgium, Eric von Ludendorff. Together they made a formidable team.

The two Russian armies were operating independently – indeed, their commanders were not on speaking terms and the bitter enemies had once even resorted to a fist fight on a public railway station. Therefore, Hindenburg and Ludendorff felt that although their forces were numerically inferior the Russians could be taken on separately.

The Germans fell first on Samsonov's army, on 29 August, and utterly destroyed it at the Battle of Tannenberg. They took over 90,000 prisoners, the Russian commander shooting himself in the wake of the defeat. The campaign against the more skilful and tactically adept Rennenkampf took longer, a series of battles and skirmishes unravelling along the Masurian lakes, but eventually Hindenburg and Ludendorff were successful and the Russian threat was nullified.

These early campaigns in the east did much to ensure the reputation of Hindenburg and, in particular, of Eric von Ludendorff.

The Russians had rather more success against Austria. When they invaded Galicia they found the terrain difficult and the campaign, spread over miles of tough country, was a confused and unmanageable one. In the wide open spaces of the region there was much marching and counter marching and casualties on both sides were heavy.

In the end, however, by sheer weight of numbers, the Russians came out on top and by October 1914 Galicia was in their hands. Russian troops soon reached the Carpathian Mountains and the day was only saved for Austria by the despatch of German troops to shore up their battered forces.

The Austrians, like Germany, had found themselves engaged in a war on two fronts – against Russia and Serbia. Unfortunately for the Austrians they were not so well prepared and the war against Serbia did not go quite as they had planned. The Serbs simply waited until the enemy lines of communication and supply were fully extended and then attacked. The Austrians were forced to retreat to the Serbian border in disarray and there, for the moment, the matter rested.

Russian Red Cross workers using sledges to bring in wounded men. The Russians were used to fighting in severe cold and snow but it did not help them against Hindenburg and Ludendorff.

GUERRE 1914-1915. — *Artillerie Russe traversant une rivière.*
Visé Paris n° 180   *Russian Artillery going through a river.* — *LL.*

A Russian artillery unit fords a river during one of the interminable battles on the Eastern Front.

The War at Sea

The war at sea began badly for Britain. On the opening day of the conflict the cruiser *Amphion* was mined off the Thames Estuary and sunk. She was closely followed by the old armoured cruisers *Aboukir*, *Hogue* and *Cressy*, all torpedoed and sunk by U9 on the same day, 22 September. Seven days later the battleship *Audacious* hit a mine and also went to the bottom.

This was a new style of warfare, where mines could be laid indiscriminately and could cause chaos to any battle fleet. Submarines could lie hidden, waiting in the depths and when, as in the case of the three armoured cruisers, ships like the *Hogue* and *Cressy* stopped to pick up survivors from the *Aboukir* they were sitting targets.

It was not all disaster for the Royal Navy, however. On 5 August the minelayer *Konigin Luise*, the very ship that had laid the mines that sank the *Amphion*, was cornered and sunk by four British destroyers. At the end of August Admiral Beatty and his battle cruiser squadron managed to run down a German force of cruisers off Heligoland Bight. In the ensuing action three enemy light cruisers were sunk.

Early the following year Beatty again intercepted raiding German battle cruisers. At the Battle of Dogger Bank the armoured cruiser *Bluecher* was crippled and sunk and, while the German battle cruisers managed to escape, the new *Seydlitz* was badly damaged. Beatty's *Lion* also suffered heavy damage but it had been a resounding victory for the Royal Navy. [9]

When the threat of German U Boats led to the Grand Fleet being moved to Ireland for its own safety, the Germans seized the initiative and twice bombarded towns on the east coast of Britain. The damage was not great, a few windows broken in Hartlepool, Scarborough and Whitby and several people killed, but the psychological effect was huge – the sanctity of the British homeland had been shattered.

The German battle cruiser *Goeben*, accompanied by the light cruiser *Breslau*, was in the Mediterranean at the start of hostilities but, despite the watchfulness of the Royal Navy, the two ships managed to slip through the Dardanelles into Constantinople. At that stage Turkey was still neutral and the ships should have been impounded. However,

Above left: HMS *Amphion*, the first British warship to be lost during the war. This view shows her minutes after she has been launched at Pembroke Dockyard in South Wales.

Above right: When German battle cruisers shelled Scarborough it was a terrifying moment for the British people. They had always believed themselves to be immune and safe from attack – now, suddenly, they were not.

The battle cruiser *Princess Royal*, one of the ships involved in the Dogger Bank battle.

a secret alliance had already been concluded between Germany and Turkey and the Turks simply stated that they had 'bought' the two ships. The ruse fooled nobody, particularly as the German crews remained on board, and shortly after, in November, the *Goeben* led a Turkish fleet in a bombardment of Odessa and other Black Sea ports. Within days Turkey came into the war on the German side.

Commerce raiders proved to be a particularly difficult problem for the Royal Navy in the early months of the war, vessels like the *Karlsruhe* and *Koenigsberg* causing havoc before they were finally eliminated. The light cruiser *Emden* was a real thorn in the British side, roaming the Indian Ocean under the command of Captain Muller and destroying Allied merchant shipping, seemingly at will, for over three months. She was eventually hunted down and destroyed off the Cocos Islands by the Australian cruiser *Sydney* on 9 November. [10]

The German High Seas Fleet remained resolutely in port at Kiel but there was one German squadron operating in the southern oceans in the early days of the war. Commanded by Admiral Count von Spee, this squadron had begun the war in Chinese waters but soon crossed to the Pacific where the hunting was better and prizes far more likely.

The German fleet consisted of four ships, including the modern armoured cruisers *Scharnhorst* and *Gneisenau*. On 1 November 1914, this squadron ran into an inferior British force off Coronel in Chile. The British Admiral, Christopher Craddock, unwisely decided to give battle, his old cruisers being outgunned and outlined against the setting sun, therefore offering perfect targets for the German gunners. Two British ships, the *Good Hope* and the *Monmouth*, were lost with all hands, including Craddock himself.

The Admiralty at once despatched two battle cruisers to the area, the *Invincible* and *Inflexible*, under the command of Admiral Doveton Sturdee. That December the British fleet was lying at anchor in Port Stanley on the Falkland Islands when a lookout spotted smoke on the horizon – von Spee, looking for further successes, had come, intending to attack Port Stanley. Instead, he had been trapped and in the battle that followed, the Battle of the Falkland Islands, his fleet was utterly destroyed. In the best traditions of the German Navy, von Spee went down with his ship. [11]

An artist's impression of the end of the raider *Emden*.

The Battle of the Falkland Islands was the first British naval success of the war. This rather romanticised artist's impression shows the end of von Spee's flagship *Scharnhorst*.

Trench Warfare

As 1914 drew to a close the pattern of the war had already been mapped out. It was to be a war of hard pounding where defence was always superior to attack. No matter where a breach was made, reinforcements could be quickly and easily assembled and moved into position. Frontal attacks on well defended positions where artillery and machine guns could dominate the battlefield were both costly and suicidal. The trouble was, the generals failed to realise it.

Trenches were an essential feature of defensive warfare, having been used in sieges for hundreds of years. The difference now was that, by Christmas 1914, a continuous line of entrenchments stretched for over 450 miles across the body of Europe and unlike a medieval siege these fortifications were occupied for four years of continuous warfare.

In most cases, soldiers dug down six or seven feet in order to create shelter. In some parts of Flanders where the water table was just too high they did not dig, they simply built up breastworks behind which they could lie. Water was a constant problem, more so in the British lines than in the Germans, which tended to be laid out on higher ground and, as a result, the trenches had to be continuously pumped out. When the Germans pumped the water out of their trenches it simply ran down the hill into British positions, an unexpected but welcome bonus for them. Digging and pumping out trenches was hard, unyielding work that, in the winter months, saw men constantly wet and covered in mud:

'I have not known what it is to have a dry foot for eight days for it has been raining day and night. The trenches get flooded and in places we have to be over our knees in water and mud. Our sleeping places get very wet.'
(Private Frank Pope) [12]

Sometimes the front lines simply disappeared under water. However, as the year wore on better pumps were employed and soldiers learned how to make and use duckboards to cover the sump or drainage ditch at the bottom of the trench in order to keep their feet out of the mud. Trenches were revetted with wood, planks or long stretches of timber that were kept in place by angle irons or simple stakes.

Gradually a complete and intricate trench system was created, crawling like crooked spiders webs across the land – front line, support trenches and a reserve line, all joined together by communication trenches that enabled men to go to and from the front line without undue risk of being shot. Fire steps lined the front wall of the trench and dug outs provided a degree of shelter for the troops. Sandbags protected the parapet (in front) and parados (behind) and, of course, the whole system was guarded by yards and yards of single strand barbed wire.

Beyond the wire lay the open killing ground of No Man's Land and beyond that again the enemy trenches. Sometimes No Man's Land was as much as a mile wide; sometimes barely fifty yards and then soldiers on both sides could hear men talking in the opposite trenches. Cratered from shell bursts – usually half full of stinking water – littered with discarded equipment and even dead bodies, No Man's Land soon came to symbolise the stupidity and futility of war, perhaps even more so than the trenches themselves.

The popular preconception is of men living in the trench system for weeks, months, even years on end, fighting battles and charging across No Man's Land every single day. Nothing could be further from the truth. Life in the trenches was thoroughly unpleasant but it was also a time of unremitting boredom, occasionally alleviated by trench raids and attacks on the enemy lines. Soldiers generally worked to the premise that if they did not annoy the Germans, then the Germans would not annoy them.

A regular system of relief was in place, units rarely spending more than a fortnight in the lines. The rest of the time they were out 'resting', a euphemism for training, practising assaults and carrying supplies up to the front. Time out of the lines was also the period when the soldiers could delouse themselves and their clothing – living in ditches dug out of the earth it was inevitable that lice, fleas and other verminous creatures proliferated.

Using Territorials and Reservists to fill the gaps, by the end of the year the BEF had been extended into two powerful units, 1st Army under Sir Douglas Haig and 2nd Army under Sir Horace Smith-Dorrien. The BEF, still under the overall command of Sir John French, now numbered more than 270,000 men.

It was not just British soldiers serving in France. The Empire responded as enthusiastically to the call as Britain herself and thousands of young colonials were soon in the trenches alongside the Scots, cockneys, Welsh and Irish that made up the bulk of the British Army. They came in boat loads from across the oceans, eager young men coming to a land and a war that were already beyond all comprehension.

Eventually, nearly 400,000 Canadians would serve in France and other theatres, 300,000 Australians and 90,000 New Zealanders, while the Indian Army sent 160,000 men. Yet that was in the years to come. As 1914 drew to a close the war still seemed a relatively parochial affair.

The Christmas Truce of 1914

The sudden and unexpected Christmas Truce of 1914 took everyone, not least the soldiers themselves, by surprise. Since the trench system had been first established

Life in the trenches – British soldiers prepare themselves breakfast after the long night.

Soldiers occupy a sap, an advance position reaching out into No Man's Land.

German soldiers, complete with one of the most effective weapons of the war – the shovel.

No Man's Land after a battle, littered with corpses and lost equipment – a killing ground if ever there was one.

In certain parts of Flanders the water table was too high to allow effective trenches to be dug. Then there was no alternative but to build a breastwork of sandbags for men to shelter behind – as shown here. Note the duckboards for walking on. In winter these would disappear under two or three feet of water.

Delousing uniforms and blankets, somewhere in France.

there had often been small scale truces, both sides, perhaps, making an unwritten and informal decision not to fire during meal breaks or when rations were being carried up. But this was something very different.

That first Christmas of the war food and gift parcels were sent by families and friends to virtually all of the soldiers and each Regiment had laid plans to celebrate with a good Christmas dinner. If a unit was in the front line on Christmas Day then celebrations would have to be delayed until they were relieved but, even so, Princess Mary's Gift Tins were freely distributed to all of the troops. Smokers received a tin containing an ounce of tobacco, twenty cigarettes, a pipe and a photograph of the Princess. Non-smokers were given the same tin but this time it contained sweets and a writing case. Many soldiers quickly sent the tins home for safe keeping, with the result that large numbers have survived, most of them without their contents.

There was a sharp frost along most of the front that Christmas Eve. As darkness fell, firing died away and lights began to appear above the German trenches, lanterns tied to

One King, One Flag, One Empire – a postcard showing all the dominion soldiers fighting for the Allies.

Indian soldiers fought, largely, in Palestine and Mesopotamia but they also came to France where the weather would have confused them totally.

the end of long poles. Then the Germans began to sing, Christmas carols and hauntingly beautiful songs about home, and soon there was widespread banter and Christmas wishes being shouted about between the men on either side of No Man's Land. [13]

The next day, on various parts of the line, soldiers called out to each other not to fire. Slowly, men began to appear on the skyline, walking cautiously towards each other. They met in the middle of No Man's Land, exchanged pleasantries and mementos and, in one place, even played a knock-up game of football – not a formal match, as has sometimes been claimed. Sometimes the informal truce lasted a few hours, at other times and in other places it went on all day.

In many places soldiers took the opportunity to bury their dead. In others, officers on both sides made a careful but discreet note of enemy dispositions. The truce was not universal, however, and on some parts of the line the war continued as normal. When news of the truce reached senior officers in their headquarters at the rear there was a furious reaction. The thought of soldiers deciding for themselves not to fight, albeit for such a short period, was totally unacceptable. Who knew where such socialist ideas might end?

A German army order for 29 December made it clear that any sort of fraternisation with the British or French would be regarded as high treason, while General Smith-Dorrien quickly announced that any officer or NCO allowing friendly contact with the enemy would find themselves facing a court martial. Again, the response was not universal. Major General Sir Thompson Capper of the 7th Division actually sanctioned a continuation of the truce on 26 and 27 December in order to bury the dead and improve drainage in the trenches.

In general, however, the truce lasted just one day. On Boxing Day, the war began again and death and mayhem descended once more across the Western Front. Orders soon came from High Command on both sides of the lines that such an event must never be allowed to happen again. In reality, it was never likely. By Christmas 1915, bitterness and even hatred had settled over both armies and the opportunity for such a peace was lost forever.

Above left: The Christmas Box given by Princess Mary to all British troops. A handsome gift; many are still to be found, nearly a hundred years after the first Christmas of the war.

Above right: German and British soldiers gather in No Man's Land during the Christmas Truce of 1914. They were wary of each other but the unofficial truce held until the next day.

1915 – And So It Goes On

New Year, 1915

While soldiers in some sections of the line reached an informal agreement with their opposite numbers that there would be a truce on New Year's Day, similar to the one at Christmas, such arrangements were rare and, ultimately, did not come to anything, thanks to the various missives from High Command. For the Germans, however, New Year meant the feast day of St Sylvester and it did, at least, ensure a few quiet days in the trenches when there was limited action and little firing.

For some soldiers the muted New Year celebrations were more memorable than the famous Christmas Truce. Private Frank Pope, later to become one of the casualties of war, wrote home about the moment when 1914 changed into 1915:

> 'At midnight on New Years Eve we could hear them (the Germans) singing and cheering, with their band playing all the time. We were only 300 yards from them and at twelve-o-clock we started as well. We were singing to them and they to us ... the Germans have got "Tipperary" off to a treat. It was all finished up with us singing the old year out and the new one in but instead of bells we had our rifles and they had theirs ... I hope I won't see the next year in here for I hope the world will be at peace before then.' [14]

The coming of the New Year, however, brought little respite. The weather was bad, trenches flooded and men continued to die. Back home in Britain, volunteers continued to besiege the recruiting offices. Many towns and cities pooled their volunteers into Pals Battalions, units made up almost entirely of men from the same area or profession or even the same street. The organisers were working on the assumption that these young men would train and fight better if they did so together. They conveniently forgot that they could also die together as well.

It was not just Pals Battalions that were forming. As the casualties in the ranks of the Old Contemptibles, the old professional British Army, became known, it was obvious that more men were needed to fill the gaps. Increasingly, men joined the army and, after training, found themselves posted to one famous Regiment after another, as replacements. A huge war machine, demanding more and more raw material – men – had been created and, at times, it seemed insatiable.

Above left: New Year 1915 did not see a continuation of the Christmas Truce, as many had expected. In some parts of the line there was no firing but nobody climbed out of their trenches to talk to men on the other side.

Above right: An artillery shell explodes behind the lines.

Life in the Trenches

Life in the trenches was cheap. Death was ever present. It could come suddenly, in the crash of an artillery shell or a rapid burst of machine gun fire. It could come during one of the many trench raids ordered by High Command, raids that were supposedly designed to gain information about units in the line opposite. In reality, their main purpose was to ensure troops retained the 'offensive spirit' – there was going to be no repetition of the Christmas Truce.

As far as the British were concerned, the standard infantry weapon of the war was the Short Magazine Lee Enfield rifle but this was of little use in trench raids. Despite the cold-blooded enthusiasm of instructors back in the training units, the bayonet was also soon found to be far less useful than had been imagined. Hand grenades, originally home-made affairs created out of jam tins but soon to be properly manufactured Mills Bombs, and coshes lovingly fashioned out of wood and nails, were far more effective when involved in trench raiding. They were brutal weapons that could murder or maim in a second.

The one weapon that everyone feared – although, ultimately, it killed far less men than artillery – was the machine gun. The machine gun had been invented by Richard Gatling in America in the 1860s, being refined and developed by Hiram Maxim twenty years later. The Vickers and Lewis guns used by British forces during the war were, really, only variations on Maxim's gun.

Despite the opinion of Sir Douglas Haig, who felt that two machine guns per Battalion were more than enough – Kitchener thought there should be four – the infantry commanders at the front knew the value of the weapon. By the time the war ended every British Battalion on the Western Front had been issued with no less than forty machine guns.

During the day, life in the trenches was relatively low-key. Morning Stand-to took place at dawn, the whole Battalion coming to awareness, ready for any possible attack.

Trench digging, always trench digging. This shows new recruits digging trenches in the Cotswolds, outside Cheltenham.

62. BRITISH MACHINE GUNNERS WEARING GAS HELMETS.

OFFICIAL PHOTOGRAPH.
CROWN COPYRIGHT RESERVED.

Two of the new weapons of the war are shown here on this early postcard view of the conflict – the machine gun dominates the scene but notice also that the men are wearing early gas masks.

1914... Boucherie de Campagne
1914... A field Meat store

Food for the soldiers. Preparing meals for the troops was never an easy task and was usually totally unappreciated by the men themselves.

This was followed by breakfast. Like all meals in the front line it was a makeshift affair, soldiers cooking tinned bacon and brewing tea on tiny 'Tommy Stoves'. Field kitchens tended to remain in reserve areas, used when a Battalion was out of the line, offering soldiers a staple diet of stew. When the cooks were able to send food up to the line it was often cold and almost inedible.

The rest of the day was spent on fatigues, cleaning the trench areas, on rifle inspections and enjoying as much free time as men could garner. They wrote letters home and kept as secure as they possibly could. A head above the parapet could easily mean death from a sniper's shot but, for those who knew how to exploit the system, there were also decided benefits. There are recorded instances of soldiers deliberately holding their hands up in the air, above the sandbags that lined the front of every trench. A bullet through the palm was a guaranteed 'Blighty Wound' and a trip home for a few months. The thought of a Blighty One was all that kept many soldiers sane. As the poet Robert Service wrote:

> I'm goin' 'ome to Blighty: can you wonder as I'm gay?
> I've got a wound I wouldn't sell for 'alf a year o' pay. [15]

Rations were brought up to the lines each night although supplies were often interrupted by shelling and enemy raids. Nevertheless, night time was when the lines really came alive, men creeping from their holes in the ground, their dugouts and trenches, to carry out trench raids and repair the wire or the trenches themselves. It was a troglodyte existence where the normal daily routines had been totally reversed.

With the coming of night came artillery shells, huge detonations that split the air and lit the sky in red, gold and orange flashes as bright as day. Flares illuminated No Man's Land and the rat-a-tat-tat of machine guns on the traverse was a constant rhythm in everyone's ears. Raiding parties inched across the mud, screams and the crump of hand grenades telling where and when they had made their mark. Only with dawn did activities begin to quieten and die away.

Foot inspection! As the caption to the postcard says, 'Making sure of their soles.' There was a serious side to the photograph – feet had to be kept in good condition, particularly in the mud and wet of Flanders. Sadly, trench foot did come to afflict many front line soldiers.

A comic postcard by F. Mackain showing the confusing nature of the trench system. Men could and did get totally lost.

Another Mackain card, this one showing soldiers out of the line on rest.

British and Australian troops load a Stokes mortar.

Artillery

Artillery barrage accounted for more deaths on the Western Front than any other weapon – even though in the early years the quality of both gunnery and of shells was remarkably poor.

In 1914 and 1915, the French had, probably, the best artillery weapon in the world. This was the 75 mm field gun but to begin with there were limited numbers available. The British equivalent was the 12 pounder while the German Army was equipped with the 77 mm field gun which fired a shell that the British promptly christened a 'whiz bang'. Mortars were employed by both sides, the British using the Stokes mortar, the Germans their infamous minenwerfer. The British quickly shortened the name minenwerfer to 'minnie' and spoke almost lovingly of its capabilities. The minnie had a longer range than the Stokes but the shell travelled slowly through the air and British soldiers were able to track it on its high, looping arc. Tracking it was one thing; getting out of its way was another.

By 1914 armies on both sides were using smokeless powder in their artillery shells, something that made observation and tasks like range finding far easier. Spotting or range finding was still a manual affair, artillery officers taking up forward positions in any battle and telephoning back to the guns the effect of their firing. When they managed to find the range then artillery fire could be very accurate, but artillery was rarely used effectively as a major offensive weapon.

For most of the war, British and French generals insisted that intense bombardment was the only way to break the deadlock and, as a consequence, demanded more guns and more shells. With these they pounded German lines, particularly in the days leading up to a major offensive. The enemy barbed wire was immune to high explosive shells and, as a general rule, was left untouched. All the bombardment brought about was a mass of churned up mud between the British and German trenches, thus ensuring that any advance across the wasteland was bound to be slow and painful.

Artillery was the most potent weapon of the war – potentially, at least. When the shortage and problems about quality of shells were finally ironed out British artillery became a very effective weapon.

New Weapons – Gas

On 22 April 1915, the Germans opened an offensive that became known as the Second Battle of Ypres. Originally intended as a minor thrust to test British and French defences, the attack soon took on more serious dimensions and the weight of artillery shells falling on the town of Ypres quickly caused most of the inhabitants to leave. Until then locals on both sides of the lines had considered themselves safe, many of them continuing to tend their fields and harvest their crops while battles raged all around them. This, however, was a new style of warfare.

As sunset approached on 22 April, French troops to the north of Ypres saw a greenish mist creeping over the field towards them. Before long the soldiers – most of them French and Algerian – began to cough and choke. Poisonous chlorine gas had been released and so effective was this new weapon that it had managed, with the French streaming away from the front lines in panic, to open up a four mile gap in the Allied line.

Luckily for the Allies, the Germans had made little preparation for their own troops who would, obviously, be walking into areas that had just been infected with gas. Such gas masks as they did possess were crude in the extreme and not very effective. Despite inflicting over fifteen thousand casualties, the German assault began to falter as many of their own men became affected by the gas. A counter-attack by Canadian and British forces eventually saved the day. They had no gas masks but someone, sniffing at the gas and recognising it as chlorine, suggested improvised masks of handkerchiefs soaked in urine.

The Germans had already experimented with gas attacks on the Eastern Front, and captured prisoners from the lines opposite Ypres had spoken about cylinders of gas in the front line trenches. Yet despite this the new weapon came as a complete surprise. Seeing its effect, both sides quickly began to use chlorine gas in large quantities. Soon other types of gas were also in use. Phosgene was employed to seep through the early masks while the most deadly of them all, mustard gas, was introduced in 1917.

After its initial success gas was never again quite so formidable. Its greatest drawback, of course, was that its use depended on the wind. If it was against you, the gas could not be released. If the wind changed direction there could be very serious repercussions as the gas blew back over the very men who had released it in the first place. Its greatest asset was the psychological factor. Men on both sides lived in terror of a gas attack, knowing it could kill, maim and have many long term effects.

New Weapons – Aircraft

When war broke out in 1914 there were very few aircraft available to any of the great nations and it would be fair to say that none of the opposing nations were ready and prepared for war in the air. The Royal Flying Corps, still an integral part of the British Army, had been formed in 1912 with the sole purpose of carrying out reconnaissance of enemy forces and positions, but when its planes flew to France in the first days of the war there were just forty-eight of them. The situation in France and Germany was basically the same although the French could summon up 136 aircraft and the Germans a total of approximately 180.

French soldiers trying on masks, goggles and blindfolds – early versions of the gas mask.

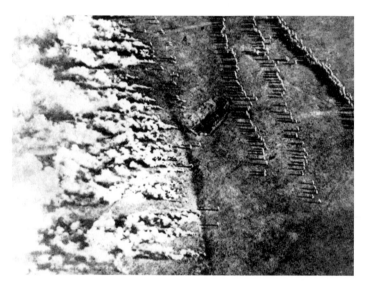

Gas was a new terror weapon, first used by the Germans on the Eastern Front and then at the Second Battle of Ypres. The Allies quickly followed suit and by the end of 1915 both sides were releasing gas canisters. The effectiveness of gas was heavily dependent on the weather – the wind had to be blowing in your favour, as this photograph clearly shows.

French troops were taken by surprise by the first use of gas. Neither they nor the attacking Germans had any idea about gas masks and for some time afterwards the most effective protection was to urinate on your handkerchief and hold it to your face.

Reconnaissance was the sole purpose of the Royal Flying Corps – at least in the beginning. This early aerial photograph is a classic example of what was produced and given to the generals to help them plan their campaigns. It was taken by a British observer in 1915.

Above left: An early British aeroplane over the trenches.

Above right: Observation balloons were another way of gaining information about enemy movements. The saying 'Everything's gone pear shaped' comes from these balloons. Filled with hydrogen they had to be inflated properly, otherwise all the gas would rush to one end of the balloon, making it shaped like a pear.

In August 1914, the RFC had four squadrons, mainly Maurice Farman Shorthorns and Longhorns and early versions of the BE2. At first the RFC was treated with scepticism and, said some commanders, the damned aircraft would do little more than frighten the cavalry horses. But the value of aerial reconnaissance was proved when early reports on the change of direction of von Kluck's drive on Paris were sent to army headquarters. So successful were these observation reports that Sir John French was moved to write a glowing tribute to the work of the RFC. With the trench line established, the RFC was at last able to operate from fixed and secure bases and aerial warfare moved on apace. [16]

The value of reconnaissance and spotting of artillery fire were realised, not just by the generals but by the enemy as well. If there were aeroplanes up over the trenches then they needed to be destroyed before they could relay their vital information back to base. And that meant anti-aircraft fire and, inevitably, fighter planes whose aim was to destroy the slow moving spotter aircraft. When more fighters were deployed to shoot down the fighters it brought about the beginning of dog fighting in the skies above France and Belgium. Early aerial combat took place with pistols and rifles but soon someone had the bright idea of mounting machine guns so that observers could fire at enemy planes. It was a revolutionary move.

As 1915 ground on, air fighting became the norm rather than an exception. Major Lanoe Hawker won the first air VC of the war in July 1915 when he shot down two enemy planes and forced a third to surrender and land – all within the space of a single day. The most important British aeroplane of the time was the Vickers Gunbus, a pusher craft with the propeller behind the pilot, thus allowing an open field of fire from the observer's Lewis gun set in the front cockpit.

A real leap forward was achieved when Dutchman Anthony Fokker offered his designs and services to the German High Command. The British and the French could also have secured Fokker's services but had turned him down. Only the German High Command was far sighted enough to realise what the little Dutchman could bring to their war effort. [17]

The result was the Fokker Eindekker, a single winged scout plane that, due to Fokker's interrupter gear, was able to fire forward through the propeller. Using this revolutionary aircraft and firing mechanism German pilots like Oswald Boelcke and Max Immelmann were soon causing chaos in the air forces of France and Britain.

New Weapons – Zeppelins

It was not just fixed wing aircraft that were causing problems for the Allies in 1915. The first Zeppelin raid on England took place on 19 January 1915 when two airships dropped bombs on Great Yarmouth. Four people were killed, sixteen were injured and there was some limited damage to property. The physical results of the raid might have been minimal but, almost immediately, the giant airships struck terror into the hearts of the civilian population.

Soon more raids were taking place on towns and cities across the country, London being subjected to its first raid in May. And as the bomb aimers became more proficient,

916. La Grande Guerre 1914-15-16 - Le dernier monoplan de Vedrine.   Visé Paris 916

IMP. BAUDINIÈRE, NANTERRE   « PHOT-EXPRESS »

Above left: Bomb damage after a Zeppelin had raided London. Broken windows and shrapnel pitted walls were one thing – soon civilian deaths would occur and the night raiders would become feared throughout the country.

Above right: A Morane Saulner Scout, the type of aircraft used to attack the early Zeppelins.

U Boats proved to be a real menace during the war years. This shows UC5 after her capture by the Royal Navy.

the damage grew. Perhaps more importantly, the psychological effect of the raids was immeasurable. This was the British homeland that was under attack and public opinion was outraged.

There was also the very real fear that one day Zeppelins might even drop gas bombs on the country. Places on the flight path of approaching Zeppelins were forced to inaugurate Britain's first 'black out', turning out street and house lights in an effort to confuse the pilots.

In 1915, these massive airships seemed invincible. German High Command quickly decided that attacks on cities, unless they were industrial centres intent on war production – which most large cities were – should be avoided. It meant that bombs were regularly dropped on British towns. Nothing, it seemed, could stop the Zeppelins. Filled with hydrogen, artillery or anti-aircraft shells could pass through the gas bags without setting the machines alight. They were big and ponderous and, in 1915, they created a reign of terror in Britain.

Zeppelin bombing of Britain stopped after 1916, when the British finally began to shoot down the huge, cumbersome beasts. The raids were not over, however, as bombing from fixed wing aircraft, the enormous Gotha bombers, continued. In all, nearly 1,100 civilians in Britain died from air attack during the war.

New Weapons – Submarines and Mines

Perhaps the most effective of all the new weapons of the war was the submarine. Although Britain employed submarines, sinking many ships close to the enemy coast, it was Germany that quickly realised the value of submarine attack, against both naval and merchant vessels. Before 1915 was out, fear of this new terror weapon was universal and German U Boats were considered as great a scourge as the Zeppelins. They demonstrated to the British public that Germany would stop at nothing to win the war.

Firing torpedoes from below the waves, it was impossible to give a warning to vessels about to be attacked. Unless the immediate area was clear of other ships – when the U Boat might attack from the surface or, afterwards, come up to offer provisions and help – the crews and passengers from the sunken vessels would have to be left to fend for themselves in open boats. It was a hard, cruel war.

Originally intended as a scouting vessel or possibly as a threat to scare off heavy battleships, the offensive value of the U Boat was demonstrated early in the war by the sinking of several British cruisers. The cruising range of these U Boats was not great and they all moved much quicker on the surface than they did when submerged. But when below the water they were a hidden and potentially devastating weapon, against which there seemed, in the early days of the war, to be no defence.

Another hidden new weapon, equally as dangerous as the submarine, was the mine. In fact, the mine was not new. Examples have been found in sixteenth-century China and Queen Elizabeth was even presented with plans for a defensive minefield in 1574. What was new was the extent of mine use in the Great War.

It is estimated that 190,000 mines – self contained explosive devices intended to sit in the water until struck by a ship – were laid in the North Sea during the war, mainly

Mines were the silent killers of the war. Nobody knew where they lay, everybody knew about their power.

by Britain. The Dover Straits, and therefore the English Channel, was heavily mined during the war in an effort to keep U Boats and enemy destroyers at bay. Germany laid mines in shipping lanes and, in the early days, had several successes. The problem with mines was that they were indiscriminate. If they were moored to the sea bed in a defensive field, people knew where they were. Mines dropped by submarines or by converted minelayers would float and could destroy friend or foe equally as efficiently.

Mine sweepers, often trawlers made of wood, were employed to sweep for mines. Once cut free from their moorings with a new device called a parvane, the mines were usually destroyed by rifle fire. It was hard, exacting work and the threat of sudden death was always present.

Battles of 1915

Moltke had been dismissed as Chief of the German General Staff in September 1914, the Kaiser appointing Erich von Falkenhayn in his place. Deciding that it would be impossible to turn the British French lines, he fixed on a largely defensive or holding war in the west while he tried to break the Russians in the east. That left the French and British to take the offensive.

The French launched a major attack in the Champagne area of the country in February 1915. It was a disaster. In a period of exactly one month they captured 500 yards of ground at the cost of 50,000 casualties.

At the Battle of Neuve Chapelle, which began on 10 March, the BEF achieved some initial success. The British had managed to assemble a huge force of artillery, having one gun for every six yards of front, but there was a major problem with shell shortage. At this time Britain was producing just 22,000 shells per day (compared to Germany's 250,000), the problem being due partly to obsolete machinery and partly the attitude of the munitions workers who felt that if the government wanted more shells they should pay more money.

British infantry
charges over the top.

As a result of the shortage the preliminary bombardment at Neuve Chapelle was limited to just four hours and was hugely effective. It was a tactic that was soon forgotten, only to be revived later in the war. At Neuve Chapelle, British forces quickly gained 1,000 yards from the Germans before the attack bogged down, sustaining over 10,000 casualties in the process.

The purpose of the Neuve Chapelle attack had been to capture the village and thus allow a second assault on Aubers Ridge. Unfortunately, the Neuve Chapelle action alerted the Germans about what was to come and that section of the line was quickly reinforced. When the assault was launched on Aubers Ridge on 9 May, an action designed to support a French attack further south, it met with severe resistance and another 10,000 casualties were recorded.

On the Eastern Front, in line with Falkenhayn's strategy of taking Russia out of the war first, the plan for 1915 was a joint attack by the Austrians through Galicia, while Hindenburg and Ludendorff advanced in the north. The Austrian attacks soon stalled but Hindenburg was more successful. In his January offensive, poisonous gas was actually used for the first time, the village of Bulimov being inundated by chlorine shells. The freezing cold conditions prevented the gas spreading and it had little effect. Tragically, the Russians failed to inform their allies about the new weapon, thus allowing the gas attack on Ypres later in the year to come as a total surprise.

In February, at the Winter Battle of Masuria where fighting took place in thick snow, Hindenburg was even more successful. He inflicted 100,000 casualties on the Russians and took even more prisoners. In an effort to shore-up the struggling Austrians in the south, German efforts now switched to Galicia where the Russians were already reaching for the Carpathian Mountains. When von Mackensen smashed the Russian Army in a two day offensive he had effectively ended the danger of any Russian invasion of Germany.

The war in the east was far from over, however. By now, Russia had mobilised over six million men – even though they had rifles for barely half that number and soldiers on the battlefield were forced to pick up and use the weapons of their dead or wounded

The devastation after a bombardment and assault can be clearly seen in this photograph from 1915. It shows captured German positions, although the trench itself has almost disappeared under the weight and ferocity of the bombardment. The sandbags, used to cushion the blast of shells and protect men from rifle fire can, however, clearly be seen.

A German trench in the winter of 1915. The wooden firing step, sandbags and wicker fence give the trench a sense of order and purpose that were, somehow, missing from British trenches of the same period.

Another German trench, this one shown after the battle. The trees beyond the trench have been shattered and there seems to be a real sense of destruction hovering in the air.

German soldiers on the Eastern Front, pulling their artillery piece through the thick snow.

Съ театра войны. Плѣнные австрійскіе офицеры.

Russian soldiers, commandeering a lift to the front.

colleagues. Russia had vast untapped resources, manpower in particular, and the war on the Eastern Front would continue to rumble on, bloody and vicious, for another two years.

The Gallipoli Campaign – Phase One

As early as December 1914 Winston Churchill had been advocating the opening of another front. Nothing was done. However, when the hard-pressed Russians asked for British intervention in the Eastern Mediterranean – an attack to distract the lurking Turkish wolf – Churchill and Jacky Fisher, then First Sea Lord, thought something might be done in the Dardanelles Straits, the narrow waterway connecting the Mediterranean to the Black Sea. Fisher's support was lukewarm; he preferred a landing

Above left: A W. L. Wyllie painting that shows the Allied bombardment of the Turkish forts during the opening phase of the Gallipoli Campaign.

Above right: A caricature of German general Liman von Sanders, one of the main architects of the Turkish defence in the Dardanelles.

in Pomerania, 100 miles north of Berlin. However, he and his civilian chief took the idea to Prime Minister Asquith and it was agreed. An assault would be made on the Dardanelles. [18]

Forcing the Dardanelles Straits would free the waterway for Allied shipping, it would cripple Turkey and it would allow attacks to be made on the soft underbelly of Austria and, therefore, on Germany as well. Attractive as that might seem, the entrance to the Dardanelles was covered by a huge array of guns, minefields and searchlights. Further batteries of guns lined the cliffs right the way along and with the width of the Channel at its narrowest point being just 1,600 yards this was always going to be a dangerous operation.

From the beginning, the campaign was a disasterous muddle. Churchill was convinced that the Royal Navy could destroy the forts without any assistance. Indeed, they had already been bombarded in November 1914, an action that had no effect other than to alert the Turks of what was to come. Further bombardments took place on 19 February 1915 and this time many of the forts were destroyed. Marines landed to mop up the dazed Turkish soldiers and to blow up any remaining defence works.

And there things stopped. Amazingly, despite the success of the operation, nothing happened for another month. The defenders on shore – German General Liman von Sanders and Mustafa Kemal, later Kemal Ataturk – swallowed their surprise and rushed extra forces to the area. When, in March, the naval forces moved warily down the Straits they ran into a minefield. Three battleships, old and due for scrapping, were sunk and several more were damaged. They promptly withdrew to Alexandria. This time there was a delay of two months.

The Gallipoli Campaign – Phase Two

The British Commander-in-Chief, Sir Ian Hamilton, was a patient and good natured man but he was too old and not really suited to the task. Loading and reloading the transports to his satisfaction took weeks and when his preparations were eventually complete Hamilton's five Divisions of British and Anzac troops (the Australian and New Zealand Army Corps) were matched by the six then boasted by the Turks.

Hamilton's landings at Kum Kale, Cape Helles and Anzac Cove on the western side of the Gallipoli Peninsula took the Turks by surprise. At all landing sites the troops got ashore but then they encountered fierce opposition that pinned them down on the beaches. Naval gunnery, which should have taken out many of the Turkish forts, was poor and did little to help the beleaguered soldiers. Hamilton remained on board ship, sailing along the coast between one landing site and another – out of touch with his troops and with events as they unfolded.

To relieve the pressure, another landing was made at Suvla Bay in the north of the peninsula. A group of Ghurkhas did manage to fight their way off the beach and climb to the top of the ridge where they could look down on the open waters of the Dardanelles. Gunners on the battleships offshore spotted the figures but did not believe that Allied troops could have penetrated so far inland. They promptly opened fire and the Ghurkhas were forced to retreat, back to the beach. Never again did Allied forces manage to breach the Turkish lines quite so effectively.

Men continued to live, fight and die on the Gallipoli beaches for many months, even though it was clear, almost from the beginning, that it was a hopeless exercise.

The Salonika Campaign

Bulgaria joined the war in September 1915, coming in on the side of Germany, Austria-Hungary and Turkey. Almost immediately, backed up with German troops, the Bulgarians launched an assault on Serbia.

The Allies saw the manoeuvrings in the Balkans as a direct threat on Greece, a country that was still neutral but with decided leanings towards Britain and France. A force of one French and two British Divisions was duly assembled under French General Maurice Sarrail and quickly moved from Gallipoli to Salonika (now known as Thessalonica) in order to defend and protect Greek territory.

The aim was for this Allied force to move off its beach-head, to link up with the Serbs and push back the enemy forces. Unfortunately, the Bulgarians and Germans had established a commanding position astride the main communication routes, a position from where they were eventually able to roll up the Serbian forces and push them towards the sea.

The Serbs, along with over 20,000 Austrian prisoners, fell back over rugged mountain terrain in what became an epic retreat. Over half the Serbian Army perished in the horrendous conditions before being picked up off the beaches by French boats. With their army gone, Serbia and most of the Balkans lay wide open and the Austrians quickly over-ran Montenegro.

The Anzac landings at Suvla Bay are shown here in all their chaos and confusion. Without proper landing craft it was a wonder any of the troops managed to get ashore.

1914-15 .. AUX DARDANELLES — Au retour des tranchées les soldats prennent un bain.
1914-15... IN THE DARDANELLES — Returning from the trenches the soldiers take a bath
Visé, Paris No 1257

Soldiers did at least manage some relaxation at Gallipoli. Bathing off the beaches, despite being under threat of Turkish shelling, was one way – and, of course, there was always the possibility of a Blighty Wound.

Καλοκαιρινὰ Γαλλικὶ Νοσοκομεῖα
Ἑλλάς—Grèce
Hôpitaux Français d' ête
Souvenir Salonique

The wired-in base for the Salonika Campaign, called by Germans 'the biggest internment camp in Europe'.

A Christmas card sent from the Balkans, one of many such cards produced by the troops and sent home.

The Allied army in Salonika now found itself isolated and with little purpose. However, General Sarrail dared not evacuate, knowing that would leave Greece wide open to attack. As a consequence the army simply wired itself in, hoping that its presence alone would be enough to deter an assault. It was a hard, cruel existence. In the early days troops slept in their greatcoats, lying in holes dug in the ground. By morning these coats would be full of water – and then the sun came up. Sunstroke or frostbite, they could both kill. [19]

The Germans scathingly called the Allied enclosure the biggest internment camp in Europe. They knew that valuable Allied forces were tied up here rather than fighting on the Western Front.

Italy Enters the War

On the outbreak of war, despite being a member of the Triple Alliance – Germany, Austria-Hungary and Italy – Italy announced that joining the conflict did not come within the terms of the alliance. She promptly declared herself neutral.

With both sides needing allies, as the war progressed there grew up a kind of auction process with everyone competing for the support and help of countries like Bulgaria and Italy. It was not just support, either. The French knew that a long war would exhaust their resources of manpower and industry and if Italy remained neutral she would be conserving her strength – it did not bear too much thought. The French even hired the socialist Benito Mussolini, a man who had been previously opposed to all capitalist wars, to lobby on their behalf. The Allies offered Italy land in the Austrian Tyrol, the city of Trieste and more territory in Asia Minor if she would come in on their side – rich pickings, indeed.

Most Italians were disinterested in the war but the country's leaders knew that if Italy had any real ambitions to be a great power she would have to take part in the conflict. And, on 26 April 1915, Italy signed the secret Treaty of London, promising to enter the war within the month. True to their word, on 23 May the Italian government declared war on Austria-Hungary. As yet, they did not feel able to take on the might of Germany and it was not until August 1916 that Italy finally went to war with the Germans.

Italy's border with Austria swept for 370 miles across some of the harshest and highest terrain in Europe. Austria-Hungary held all the high ground and yet this was where the Italians had to fight. It was to be one of the most vicious and deadly fronts of the whole war.

The Italians planned to invade the Austro-Hungarian plain but first they had to get over the mountains. The Battle of Isonzo, in reality eleven different but linked battles, took place between June and November 1915. Little was gained but as many as 160,000 casualties were incurred in what was little more than a bloodbath, on both sides, and here, as elsewhere, the war ground on relentlessly.

The Suez Canal

A Turkish thrust towards the Suez Canal in February 1915 caused great consternation in British ranks. Britain could not afford to lose control of the Canal as it was the main route to and from India. So, when 20,000 Turkish soldiers suddenly appeared out of the Sinai Desert, there was panic.

Luckily the attack was repulsed fairly easily. The British High Command had learned a lesson, however, and reinforcements were immediately sent to the region. In the event the Turks did not try for the Canal again for another eighteen months. They had other things on their minds.

The Turkish failure to exploit British fears about the Canal was only partially a mistake. It is doubtful if Turkey could ever have taken the waterway, certainly not once the area had been reinforced. But the cost of maintaining a garrison in this part of Egypt was immense and the soldiers who were engaged sitting on the Suez Canal, twiddling their thumbs in impatience, could and should have been more use in France. It was an interesting experience for many of the young soldiers:

> 'I'd joined up expecting to be in France, on the Western Front, in a few weeks but, instead, I found myself in Egypt. I'd read about the pyramids and now, suddenly, there they were in front of me. It was amazing. For me the most impressive thing was the Sphinx. It just sat there in the desert like a giant cat. I was shocked, taken aback. This thing had been there for thousands of years and here we were, knowing that sooner or later we would be facing death and destruction.' [20]

For most of the young soldiers Egypt was a brief interlude. Many of them soon moved on, to Gallipoli or France. For others it would be the country where they waited, impatient and frustrated, until the campaigns in Mesopotamia and Palestine began in earnest.

Mesopotamia

From the beginning of the war the British knew they would have to protect their interests – in particular, their oil interests – in the Middle East. As a result, a British

The war between Austria and Italy was long, hard and bloody. This shows a detachment of Austrian infantry with their heavy machine guns.

478. - Groupe de Chasseurs Alpins dans les Alpes

Édition Giletta, phot., Nice.

Much of the Austro-Italian war was fought in the mountains and Alpine troops were crucial in such an environment. This idyllic scene was very far from the truth.

German officers at the foot of the Carpathian Mountains. The terrain was rugged and deadly for all sides.

A British artillery unit poses alongside the Sphinx and in front of the Great Pyramid in Egypt. None of these soldiers had ever expected to see such sights.

and Indian force was landed in Mesopotamia (modern day Iraq but then part of the Turkish Empire), in the autumn of 1914. Basra was soon occupied and the decision was made to press northwards and occupy the whole country.

The British moved relentlessly onwards, easily defeating a Turkish counter attack at Nasiriya in April 1915. General Townshend reached Kut el Amira in September and took the town fairly easily. With extended lines of communication, he was dubious about pressing on but was urged to do so by the Commander-in-Chief General Dixon, back in Basra. Another victory at Ctesiphon left Townshend's force so exhausted that he had no option but to retire to Kut. And there his command of 9,000 men was instantly besieged by a vastly superior force of Turks – Townshend, like Dixon, had greatly underestimated the size and strength of the enemy.

Several attempts were made to relieve the men at Kut but all were unsuccessful. Townshend held out for several months before, in April 1916, with supplies running out he was forced to surrender. The garrison was marched off into captivity, 5,000 of the 9,000 men never being heard of again.

Things might have worked out differently had Townshend not promised to feed the civilian population of Kut as well as his own troops. Only later did it come out that, before the British forces fell back on Kut, the people of the town had buried large supplies of grain, enough to feed them and the garrison for many months. Had this been available to Townshend he could have held out and allowed the relieving forces to gather their resources and attack at their leisure.

The War in Africa

German colonies in Africa were captured quite quickly once war began, Togoland and the Cameroons being in Allied hands by the end of February 1915. The assault on German South West Africa (now Namibia) took a little longer, mainly due to a rebellion in the South African forces deployed for the campaign. This was led by men who had fought the British in the Boer War, men seeking the chance of a little revenge, and it took some time to quell. Despite this the campaign was over by July 1915, German forces surrendering to Louis Botha, another soldier who had fought for the Boers in the recent war.

For Peace at almost any Price.

JOHNNIE TURK, whose German master has let him down.

Above left: A political cartoon trying hard to tell the world that Germany has dragged Turkey into an unnecessary but costly war.

Above right: British soldiers outside their tents in Mesopotamia.

British troops at camp in Mesopotamia.

The campaign in German South West Africa was long and hard, thanks to the quality of the German and African forces involved. It kept British and Colonial troops pinned down in what was considered a 'side show' when they would have been much more useful in France.

A British ambulance wagon passes through a gully on its way to the front.

A British patrol takes a rest in the rugged terrain.

Little progress was made in East Africa, however. Here the German commander was the articulate and inventive Paul von Lettow-Vorbeck who gradually built up an army of some 25,000 Africans and Europeans. Numbers of soldiers was not his problem – he simply could not arm them appropriately. Yet the terrain over which the war was fought consisted of thick brush and von Lettow-Vorbeck's mainly African Askaris were experts in dealing with such difficult territory.

A humiliating defeat was handed out to the British when they attempted a landing at Tanga, 800 casualties being inflicted, and to make matters worse several ships carrying essential supplies managed to break the British blockade.

Finally, the government of South Africa appointed General Smuts, a guerrilla commander of some note – as the British, against whom he had fought in the Boer War, could testify – to deal with von Lettow-Vorbeck. Even so, it was not until the middle of 1916 that Dar-es-Salaam was captured and even then Von Lettow-Vorbeck escaped capture to continue the fight.

The *Lusitania* and Nurse Cavell

Early in 1915 Germany declared a blockade of the British Isles. It was a warning to all ships, of whatever nationality, that if they came within sight or range of a U Boat they would be destroyed without compunction. Calls of 'German barbarity' counted for nothing.

When the liner *Lusitania* was sighted by U 20 off the coast of Ireland in March 1915 she was too good a target to miss and a single torpedo sent her to the bottom. Ostensibly a vessel carrying just passengers, the speed with which the ship broke up and a secondary explosion on board soon after the torpedo struck does seem to indicate that she was also carrying explosives or military supplies.

Unfortunately, 1,195 men and women also went down with the *Lusitania*, 128 of them being American citizens. The Germans commemorated the event by striking a special medal – American opinion was outraged. President Wilson protested and it quickly became clear to men like the German Chancellor Theobald Bethmann-Hollweg that such indignation could even bring America into the war. As a result, the German 'sink at sight' campaign was abandoned or at least severely limited until the idea of 'total war' was adopted in 1916.

On 11 October 1915, Edith Cavell was executed by the Germans in Brussels. She had been working as the matron of Berkendael School for Nurses and here she first shielded and then helped British and French soldiers to escape to neutral Holland. Arrested and put on trial, she was condemned to death, not as a spy but as someone who had helped enemy soldiers to escape. Protests from all over the world could not save her.

The execution of Nurse Cavell brought ignominy and shame to the German nation and was fully exploited by the British press. The two events – the sinking of the *Lusitania* and the shooting of a British nurse – did much to bolster morale in a dark and deadly time of war.

Above left: The sinking of the *Lusitania* brought condemnation to the German government and almost took America into the war. Emotive postcards like this one kept up the pressure on the 'dastardly Hun'.

Above right: Nurse Cavell, shot by the Germans for helping Allied prisoners to escape – not Germany's best PR moment.

The indestructible British Tommy, out souvenir hunting – something that all troops, on both sides, did on a regular basis. They would be sent home to family or friends or sold for extra rations and beer.

The Battle of Loos

The Battle of Loos, which took place in September 1915, was undoubtedly the biggest battle that the British Army had fought, up to that time. It was also one of the biggest disasters and it spelled the end of the line for the commander of the British Expeditionary Force, Sir John French.

At 6.30 a.m. on 26 September gas was released, billowing in waves towards the German trenches, and British troops went over the top. In a swirling wind the gas drifted forward on the right but swept backwards on the left, asphyxiating many of the attacking troops. And when they reached the German lines, soldiers – most of them Territorials – found the wire uncut by the bombardment. In fierce fighting the village of Loos was taken by Haig's forces but the reserves did not appear in time and the gains were quickly lost. French, never Haig's greatest friend or colleague, simply did not trust him to use his forces appropriately and therefore kept the reserves under his own command.

Despite Haig's urgent demands for support, it was not until mid morning – and then in driving rain – that the reserves were finally released. By then the Germans had managed to regroup and the advancing men were mown down by the machine guns that simply traversed along the line of troops. In just four hours over 4,000 soldiers were killed, total British losses for the battle amounting to 43,000. Among them was Jack Kipling, son of the famous author. His body was never found and Kipling, who had used his influence to get his short sighted boy into the army, was devastated. He spent the rest of his life trying to find out more about his son's fate.

The handling of the reserves by Sir John French was severely criticised by many officers, among them Douglas Haig. He had the ear of the king and was determined that blame for the failure should lie at the door of French, not him. He also had designs on Sir John's job and even went so far as to circulate 'leaked' papers regarding French's handling of the reserves. It was underhand behaviour, even caddish, but it was successful.

With his political support waning, French's position had become untenable and he was eventually relieved in December 1915. When the reshuffling had finished French found himself replaced by none other than Sir Douglas Haig. French went, bitter and resentful, adamant that Haig had stabbed him in the back.

Sir John's Chief of Staff, Sir William Robertson, was soon promoted to become Chief of the Imperial General Staff. Robertson came from a poor background and had enlisted as a private soldier, rising through the ranks by solid determination and intelligence. He never quite mastered the English language – despite becoming fluent in several others – and constantly dropped his aitches. The story is told that when Sir John French was relieved of his command, Robertson told him bluntly 'You're for 'ome, Johnny.'

The Gallipoli Campaign – Phase Three

Despite 50,000 replacements being sent from Britain, by the autumn of 1915 it was clear that the Gallipoli campaign had turned into a disaster on a massive scale. No matter how many extra troops were sent, they were always matched by Turkish replacements and it proved impossible to get the men off the beaches.

Above left: Sir John French, who lost command of the British Expeditionary Force after the Battle of Loos – and after Douglas Haig had slipped in the knife once or twice.

Above right: Sir Douglas Haig, the arch intriguer, is shown here with some very distinguished company. From left to right – Joffre, President Poincare of France, King George V, General Foch and Haig himself.

British artillery on the Gallipoli Peninsula.

Above left: A British dressing station somewhere on Gallipoli. It seems well-ordered and calm, a far cry from the truth.

Above right: David Lloyd George, the Welsh wizard, a man whose political stock rose considerably as 1915 progressed.

Sir Ian Hamilton was relieved, replaced by General Monro, but when Field Marshal Kitchener visited the scene he was appalled by what he saw. His report back to the High Command was simple – the Gallipoli Peninsula must be abandoned and the campaign called off.

Evacuation began in December 1915 and ended, with the last troops being taken off the beach at Suvla Bay, on 9 January 1916. It was a hugely effective withdrawal, in utter contrast to the rest of the campaign. The Turks did not even realise the enemy was leaving until they woke one morning to find the beaches and trenches opposite them totally empty.

Nearly 500,000 Allied troops had been involved in the landings and occupation of Gallipoli, 250,000 of them becoming casualties. Many of those casualties came through disease rather than enemy action. It had been a disasterous campaign, from beginning to end.

In its wake Churchill was forced to resign from the Admiralty. He decided to leave government for the time being and, having served as a soldier in the Sudan under Kitchener, was able to gain a commission in the army. Within a few weeks he was in command of the 6th Battalion, Royal Scots Fusiliers, a position he held until the end of 1916 when he made the decision to come back into politics full time. Even when he was serving in the trenches Churchill remained an MP, taking time to go home on leave to speak in Parliament on the 1916 Navy Estimates, but his primary concern – one he fulfilled more than admirably – was as a line officer in an infantry regiment. He remained convinced that Gallipoli could have been a glorious victory – 'I came, I saw, I capitulated' was his final comment on the affair.

Admiral Jacky Fisher also went. Always totally sure of his own ability, he wrote a virulent letter to Prime Minister Asquith, outlining his demands, the things he would need if he was

With Lloyd George as Minister for Munitions the production of shells and guns improved drastically. It was to make a huge difference to the men at the front.

Above left: The Suffragettes had abandoned their militant campaign for the duration of the war but the Pankhursts – this shows Emmeline and Christabel leaving Bow Street Magistrates Court some years before – still wanted to work alongside men, on an equal footing. Lloyd George gave them the chance.

Above right: During the course of the Great War women gradually became employed in a wide range of jobs, everything from nursing and munitions work to farming and bus driving.

going to stay as First Sea Lord. He confidently expected the government to agree to his conditions. Travelling north to his home in Scotland he was met by the Station Master on the platform at Crewe with a telegram – Asquith had accepted his resignation. [21]

The battles on the Gallipoli Peninsula exacted a terrible cost in human life. The Anzac forces never forgave the ineptitude of the British generals, men who had condemned them to death and disaster, but for the ordinary soldier – British, Australians, New Zealanders – the real heroes of the campaign were the men who had fought and died on those terrible beaches:

> Above your graves no wattle blooms
> Nor flowers from English dells,
> You men who sleep uneasily
> Beside the Dardanelles.
> (P. MacGill) [22]

Much of the general perception about the running of the war – lions led by donkeys – comes from the sheer ineptitude of the men in charge of the Gallipoli Campaign. The idea was right, the execution totally wrong. It really was a case of 'What if?'

Change Lies in the Air

A sense of change had been ever-present for much of 1915. It wasn't just Sir John French, Churchill and Jacky Fisher who went to the wall. In the wake of many failures in France and the chaos of the Gallipoli Campaign, H. H. Asquith, the Liberal Prime Minister – the man whose supposed answer to any problem was 'Wait and see' – realised his position was tenuous. He decided that the only way forward was to form a coalition government with the Conservatives.

Lord Kitchener had been increasingly criticised for his running of the war, in particular for a serious shortage of shells for the guns in France. Now, in the new coalition government, he was to be the sacrificial lamb. He was not dismissed but his powers were severely curtailed while David Lloyd George, the Welsh wizard, became the new Minister for Munitions.

Lloyd George, the man of the people as he liked to style himself, quickly persuaded the Unions to end their restrictions on quantity of shell production. The issues of working conditions and fixed wages could be dealt with after the war, Lloyd George promised. In the meantime, let's get on with the job. Lloyd George was dynamic and often high handed but his approach was exactly what was needed at the time.

The militant suffragettes had suspended most of their political protests in 1914 but they had been demanding, for some time, the right to work alongside men. Lloyd George now gave them that right. Thousands of women were brought into the armaments factories, their smaller hands being particularly useful for reaching down inside shell casings.

Soon women were working at a whole range of jobs that had previously been closed to them. They drove buses and trams, worked on farms and delivered coal. There were even, for the first time, women police officers. As 1915 came to an end it was clear that the world had changed – and this time it had changed forever.

1916 – The Year of Slaughter

Conscription

On 6 January 1916, the British coalition government broke with hundreds of years of tradition and introduced a Bill to bring in compulsory military service for all single men. This move had little to do with the flow of volunteers as men were still coming forward by their thousand, all still eager to 'do their bit'. It was just that the government felt obliged to do more to help the progress of the war and the introduction of conscription would bring Britain into line with the other European powers.

The expected disapproval of the Liberal Party did not materialise and the Bill quickly passed through Parliament to be enshrined in law. Voluntary recruiting stopped but, rather than the half million 'shirkers' that the Act was expected to expose, almost immediately there were over a million claims from men who wanted exemption because they were engaged in essential war work.

A new phenomenon also now suddenly appeared – the conscientious objector. Now that service in the armed forces was compulsory, men were able to object to the war on moral and religious grounds. Many of these objectors refused to bear arms and fight but were happy to serve as stretcher bearers and orderlies in the dressing stations. Others wanted nothing to do with the war. There were not many of these 'conchies', as they were called, perhaps five thousand in total but, by and large, they were treated harshly by the authorities. Many of them were imprisoned for their beliefs, sentenced to hard labour in Dartmoor and other prisons.

One thing that conscription did end was under age enlistment. So many young boys – and they were just boys – had lied about their age in order to join up. When they reached the front it was only understandable when some of them were unable to cope with the shock, the horror and brutality of what they saw. In all, 346 British soldiers were shot by firing squad during the war, the vast majority (266 of them) for desertion in the face of the enemy. Conscription would not end this process but it would cut out the needless suffering of young lads whose only real mistake was that they had been 'ardent for some desperate glory'.

Once conscription had been introduced it was, perhaps, inevitable that the terms by which it operated should be extended. The original legislation had been aimed only at single men over the age of eighteen. However, in May 1916 this was extended to cover married men as well. Now the war really was touching all people, all classes and parts of society. Women, who were not forced to join the army, were encouraged to head for the factories and take the places of men who had been called up.

Above left: Conscription marked the beginning of 1916; the first time compulsory enlistment was ever introduced in Britain. It met with mixed reaction, as this postcard from the time shows.

Above right: Conscription quickly led to the new phenomenon of conscientious objectors. This unusual photograph shows a humorous response to the problem, perhaps at a fête or garden party.

New draftees being marched off to their billets.

The Battle of Verdun

By 1916 'Pappa' Joffre was the most powerful general on the Allied side. He was insistent that a joint offensive, British and French, would break the German armies and the place to unroll this attack was not in Flanders, but in the relatively unspoiled and unmarked Somme region. The area was unspoiled because it had no towns or landmarks of any particular or strategic significance but that did not matter to Joffre. Britain had not been pulling her weight, he felt, and what he wanted now was to involve Haig and his armies in heavy fighting.

Haig, acting under instructions from Kitchener, acquiesced to Joffre's request and the two generals began to plan for the attack. Unfortunately, they were forestalled as the Germans under von Falkenhayn were also planning an assault. Falkenhayn was aware of the casualties France had suffered during the past eighteen months and was convinced that if he could bleed the French Army dry then it would deprive Germany's greatest enemy, Britain, of her ally and thus shorten the war by many months, perhaps even years.

Falkenhayn needed a target that was not necessarily important from a strategic or tactical point of view but one that was a symbol, the loss of which would destroy the morale of the French nation. He found it in the fortress city of Verdun. Even though the forts of Verdun were already redundant, the French people did not realise this – to them they were a symbol of French pride and military efficiency.

The attack began on 21 February 1916, an enormous bombardment that shook the earth and could be heard fifty miles away. Siege mortars, heavy artillery, even new weapons like flame throwers were used against the French defenders. The forts and the town were reduced to rubble but the French line held. Despite the fact that Verdun was of little strategic value, Joffre ordered that there should be no retreat and thus fell happily into Falkenhayn's trap.

What ensued was a bloodbath like no other as both sides battered and fought their way to a standstill. The French commander, General Henri Petain, and his subordinate Robert Nivelle, were inspirational as, day after day, the Germans threw themselves against the defences. 'They shall not pass' was the cry, one that was willingly and eagerly taken up by the men in the trenches.

The Battle of Verdun was one of the bloodiest in the whole war. French troops withstood a terrible battering but held their ground and fought on to the death. Hardly a household in France did not have some relative killed or injured in the battle.

BATTERY OF FRENCH SEVENTY-FIVE'S AT VERDUN

French seventy-fives, the most effective short range artillery weapon of the war, moving up to the Verdun sector.

A CONVOY OF SHELLS NEARING THE BATTLE FRONT. VERDUN

French supply columns on The Sacred Way, the single road that was the only way in or out of Verdun.

THE SOLDIERS' SLEEPING QUARTERS

A French dugout, deep underground – complete with pet dog.

This was a battle of attrition where the victor would be the side who could endure the longest. To do this, supplies of weapons and reinforcements were essential. The German forces had good rail and road links behind their lines; the French had just one way into the city, a road that soon became known as La Voie Sacree (The Sacred Way). Along this 75 mile track nearly 3,000 lorries and carts passed each day, carrying 50,000 tons of munitions and supplies every week. Reinforcements, too, came along The Sacred Way – it was the only route into the city.

Fighting finally died away at the end of June and by then the French had suffered over 400,000 casualties. The Germans had lost nearly 350,000. It was a senseless battle with no objective other than to wear down the other side. In the end it was a victory, of sorts, for the French. They had, more or less, held their ground but Falkenhayn never knew how close he had come to his objective. Verdun destroyed the spirit of the French Army and the mutinies that broke out later in the year were directly related to the horror of this senseless, mindless bloodbath.

Relief for Verdun

As the battle for Verdun ground remorselessly on Joffre repeatedly sent out desperate calls for help. He did not want British, Italian or Russian troops to come to his aid, that would have been unthinkable and impracticable, but what he did want were offensives that might just distract the attention of the German High Command and even pull German troops away from the Verdun sector.

Joffre's allies tried their best to respond. The Italians launched new attacks over and around the Isonzo River but when the Austrians managed to work their way around to their rear, the Italians found themselves in serious trouble. Soon they, too, were asking for help from their allies.

The Russians launched a series of offensives on the Eastern Front, but Hindenburg and Ludendorff, warned of the attacks when copies of the Russian plans fell into their hands, were more than a match for the Czar's forces. Russian soldiers were cut down in their thousands and their sacrifice did nothing to help the French in Verdun.

The Russians were more successful in the south where the armies of General Brusilov were pitted against the Austro-Hungarians. Brusilov attacked at various points, without any preconceived plan of campaign, and the Austrians fell back in disorder. Over 250,000 prisoners were taken. The attacks did divert some forces that Falkenhayn had intended for Verdun but not enough to affect the outcome of the battle. With the more determined Germans now hammering at his forward troops, Brusilov had no option but to retreat. In the end the Russian campaign, designed purely to help the men at Verdun, cost them well over a million casualties.

And then, of course, there were Haig and the British armies. The original intention had been to launch a combined British and French offensive on the Somme. Clearly this could not now happen and Haig, bowing to pressure from 'Pappa' Joffre, agreed to mount the attack with, predominantly, just British forces.

Above left: Russian soldiers attack over snow laden and frozen ground.

Above right: The impact of high explosive shells could be traumatic. Men were maimed and killed; some were psychologically impaired for the rest of their lives; many were simply blown to atoms. This photograph gives a realistic view of the effect although some of the German soldiers seem oblivious of the shell bursting right alongside them.

The Battle of the Somme

Although originally dubious about an attack on the Somme, Haig had quickly become convinced that this undamaged and gently rolling pasture land was the very spot where the war could be won. Over a period of many weeks British forces were moved into the area, most of them men of Kitchener's New Army. This was to be their blooding and they, like Haig, were convinced that they would succeed where others before them had failed.

Quite why High Command felt so sure of success is not clear. The Germans held all the high ground and, more significantly, because there had been so little action in the area they had had the time to construct deep dugouts in the chalky soil. These dugouts made them almost immune to any type of shelling available to the British in 1916.

The attack on 1 July 1916 was preceded by a bombardment on a colossal scale, lasting for a total of five days. Observers from the Royal Flying Corps reported widespread devastation but they, and the generals, did not realise that whatever damage might be inflicted on the first and second lines of trenches, the Germans were waiting, safe and sound, underground in their deep dugouts. [23]

For several weeks, tunnelers had been digging mines under the enemy trenches – three large and seven small. Packed with explosives, these were meant to be blown at 7.28 a.m.

precisely, thus allowing two minutes for the dust and debris to settle before the infantry Battalions rushed to lips of the craters to mow down the survivors. Unfortunately, one of the mines, close to the village of Beaumont Hamel, was blown at 7.20 and the Germans were alerted. The shock of the mines exploding was almost unbelievable. The ground trembled and the shock waves knocked men off their feet. One of the largest craters, Lochnager, to the south of La Boisselle, can still be seen, a huge rent in the earth that looks like nothing more than the beginnings of a mass grave.

When the shelling stopped, the men of Kitchener's New Army went over the top, walking forward in regular lines, shoulder to shoulder, waving flags and singing their interminable soldiers songs. Each of them carried 60 lbs of equipment on his back and the ground over which they walked had been turned into a quagmire by the shelling. The barbed wire, however, remained largely uncut and this was where the German machine gunners, now up and out of their dugouts, caught them. The slaughter was appalling. As the day wore on, many of the reserves were cut down the moment they left their trenches. The attack had begun at 7.30 a.m. and before most people in Britain had even finished their breakfast over 14,000 men had been killed.

In hindsight the Somme was a disaster waiting to happen. The men of the New Army had received scant training. They knew how to walk forward in a line and how to use the bayonet on a demoralised foe and that was about it. Nobody had any idea about using initiative or operating in small groups. Their junior officers were undoubtedly brave and like their men were full of reckless enthusiasm. They had been told to lead from the front, to expose themselves to enemy fire – as an example – and so were often mown down in the first moments of the battle.

It was not all doom and gloom. Mauntauban and Mametz were captured and the Ulster Division easily reached its objective of Grandcourt, just north of Thiepval, thanks largely to the expedient of moving before the whistles blew for zero hour. From there, however, things went drastically wrong. The Ulsters waited for reinforcements that had been redirected and did not come and, eventually, were wiped out by German counter attacks.

Lochnager Crater on the Somme battlefield. It remains a fitting tribute to the victims of the Somme.

German prisoners are brought in on the first day of the Somme. These must have been some of the few – the first day of the Somme was the blackest day the British Army has ever endured, 20,000 men being killed or just vanishing without trace.

THE WILTSHIRES CHEERING DURING THE 'GREAT ADVANCE.

British troops moving up to take their place in the Battle of the Somme.

This photograph shows soldiers moving up to the front complete with barbed wire and the metal stanchions to secure it to the ground.

In the main, the first day of the Somme was an utter disaster, the worst day in the history of the British Army. The casualty figure was put at 57,470, of these nearly twenty thousand being killed. Many of the wounded were also to die in the hours and days ahead.

Once the initial shock had worn off, British High Command had to consider what to do next. So much blood had been spilled on both sides that everyone thought the Germans must be close to breaking point. Therefore the battle should continue. Over the next few months numerous attacks – all loosely grouped together under the title of the Battle of the Somme – were made on positions like Delville and Mametz Woods. The attack on Mametz Wood by the 38th (Welsh) Division was a particularly brutal affair that was meant to take less than a day. In the event the battle lasted five days and virtually destroyed the Welsh Division – Lloyd George's Division as it was known – as a fighting force. [24]

The final attack took place on 13 November, when the village of Beaumont Hamel was eventually taken, and thereafter both sides subsided into a daze of recrimination and wonder. British casualties for the battle amounted to 420,000. Even the French, who had occupied a small portion of the southern front, lost 205,000. German losses came to over 600,000. Arguably, it was ultimately a victory for the British as the vast majority of the objectives laid down by Haig and General Rawlinson, the man in direct charge of the offensive, were eventually taken. But at what cost? And the horrors of that first day can never be extinguished.

If, as has sometimes been claimed, the Somme was 'the death of an army' – meaning Kitchener's New Army – it also has to be seen as the death of the old German Army. Old values and old positions died along with the soldiers on the Somme. A newer, harsher world was about to emerge.

Rebellion in Ireland

Ireland had been close to open rebellion for several years before the war began. The question of Irish Home Rule was a thorny one that successive British governments had either failed to address effectively or had deliberately ignored. While a large number of Irishmen wanted Home Rule and were prepared to go to almost any lengths to achieve it, a significant number of men and women in the fiercely Protestant area of Ulster were equally as ready to fight to defend their loyalty and adherence to Britain and the crown.

When war broke out in 1914 most Irishmen, Protestant and Catholic, immediately rallied to the British flag. For them the issue of Home Rule was suspended until hostilities were over. However, a small number of partisans – probably less than eight or nine thousand – quickly realised that Britain, engaged in a life and death struggle with Germany, was suddenly vulnerable. This was their chance.

Sir Roger Casement, once British consul in Mozambique and the Congo, was at the forefront of events. Since his days as a Colonial administrator he had become a fanatical Irish nationalist and now he travelled to Germany – after war had broken out – in an attempt to persuade the German government to land guns in Ireland for use in a rising. Despite the seeming agreement of the Germans (the date of Easter 1916 was fixed for the rising) Casement soon realised they had no intention of helping in such a subversive and, as they saw it, underhand plot.

Disillusioned, Casement returned to Ireland, travelling in a German submarine. He was arrested within a few hours, walking on the rugged west coast of the country. Despite the protests of many influential men and women Casement was convicted of treason and hanged on 29 June 1916. The leaking of his diary by the British government, a diary which revealed that he was a homosexual with many highly placed contacts, might well have had something to do with the lack of clemency shown towards him.

Casement had come back to warn his comrades that German support would not be forthcoming. The rising was cancelled and most of the Irish Volunteers, as they were known, went quietly home to wait for the next time. In Dublin, however, a small number of rebels decided to go ahead with the rising.

Shots were fired at British sentries at Dublin Castle and on Easter Monday, members of the Irish Volunteers, supported by the Irish Citizens Army, seized strategic buildings around the city, notably the Post Office in Sackville Street. From here they proclaimed a new Irish Republic, the Proclamation being written by Patrick Pearse and James Connolly. When British troops were sent to calm the situation, fighting broke out and lasted for five days.

During the week, as news of the rising spread, the rebels were reinforced by 1,600 volunteers. Eventually almost 20,000 British troops were facing them in the Dublin streets. Artillery was brought in to bombard the Post Office and eleven people were killed before the rebels finally surrendered. By that time the Post Office was devastated and James Connolly, one of the rebel leaders, was severely injured.

In the wake of the rising, hasty trials were arranged. All seven of the main leaders, the men who had signed the Proclamation, and many of the Volunteer Commandants who led the various units were condemned and executed by firing squad. James Connolly, too badly injured to walk, was carried out into the execution yard in a chair. There is no doubt that idealists like Patrick Pearse and James Plunkett wanted death and martyrdom as, they felt, only in this way could the spirit of Irish nationalism be brought alive once more. Foolishly, the British authorities gave them what they wanted. In total, sixty-four Irish partisans lost their lives in the abortive rising, either in the fighting at the Post Office and around Dublin or as a result of what were, really, little more than 'kangaroo courts'.

The ruins of Sackville Street in the aftermath of the Easter Rising, April 1916. Despite the battle the daily routine seems to be going on as normal.

Inside the General Post Office, held by the rebels for five days and eventually bombarded by British artillery.

By executing so many of the leaders of the uprising the British government made the rebels – most of whom were unpopular at the time, even in their homeland, being viewed as unpatriotic – into heroes. In effect the British had turned Ireland into a hotbed of Republicanism and rebellion. It was something which, in years to come, would come back to haunt them, many times.

Hundreds of rebels, who had managed to escape the firing squads, men like Eamon de Valera and Michael Collins, were sent to prison camps in Britain, many of them finding their way to Frongoch Camp in North Wales. Lumped together in austere and primitive surroundings their anger and determination grew only stronger.

Total War

In the summer of 1916 German politicians decided that it might be time to seek a peace agreement with the Allies. Men such as Chancellor Bethmann-Hollweg still believed that Germany could win the war but they knew that ordinary methods and tactics would never achieve victory. The only methods likely to succeed, ideas such as unrestricted submarine warfare, were unpalatable in the extreme.

So, in December 1916, Germany presented a peace proposal at the Vatican. It was hardly calculated to find favour with the Allies, demanding, among other things, that Germany be given Belgian Congo, a restoration of all German colonies in Africa and direct control over the state of Belgium. Not surprisingly, the proposal was rejected out of hand.

In the wake of Verdun and the Somme it was clear that Falkenhayn had shot his bolt – a new approach was required. On 29 August, with both battles still raging, he was replaced as Chief of the General Staff by Paul von Hindenburg, the victor of so many campaigns on the Eastern Front. Hindenburg came accompanied by his Chief of Staff Eric von Ludendorff – and both men, militarists to the core, knew that the only route to victory was by the concept of 'total war'.

It was a concept to which Bethmann-Hollweg was utterly opposed. He was nothing if not a moderate in his approach and this inevitably brought him into conflict with von

On oublie toujours ça.

Ne sortez pas du boyau! Ils tirent sur l'ambulance.

'They shall not pass,' said General Petain but his defence of Verdun brought the French Army to its knees.

Hindenburg. With militarism clearly in the ascendancy Bethmann-Hollweg was gently eased out, his place being taken by the far more pliable but infinitely less able Georg Michaelis.

Ludendorff was undoubtedly the power behind von Hindenburg's new throne. He was sometimes known as 'Hindenburg's Brain' and was an adherent to the policies and ideas of a German general who had died as far back as 1831. This was Karl von Clausewitz, a man whose writings had only been published after his death. Von Clausewitz, who had at one time been Chief of Staff to Count Gneisenau, was clear that the only way to defeat an enemy was to smash him utterly, to grind him into the dirt – in other words, 'total war'. Now Ludendorff was about to put the ideas and theories of von Clausewitz into terrible practise.

The Battle of Jutland

It has been said that Admiral Sir John Jellicoe, commander of the British Grand Fleet, was the only man who could lose the war in a single afternoon. The responsibility of controlling and directing Britain's greatest weapon was indeed a heavy one but Jellicoe, like his German counterparts, was living and planning for the day when the two great fleets would meet in battle.

At the end of May 1916, Admiral Scheer, commander of the German High Seas Fleet, decided that he had lain inactive long enough. He duly sent out his battle cruiser squadron under Admiral Hipper in the direction of the Skagerrak Straits between Denmark and Norway, knowing that the move was bound to attract the attention of the British. Vice Admiral David Beatty, commander of the First Battle Cruiser Squadron, saw and answered the challenge.

What emerged was a massive game of cat and mouse. Scheer was hoping to lure Beatty's ships beneath the guns of his battleships – Jellicoe, thundering in the wake of Beatty's battle cruisers, was hoping to catch the Germans in their own trap. There had never been a greater gathering of warships. On the British side there were twenty-eight dreadnought battleships, nine battle cruisers and over 120 smaller vessels. The German High Seas Fleet consisted of twenty-two battleships, five battle cruisers, eleven cruisers and sixty-one destroyers. Potentially, at least, it was Armageddon waiting to happen.

Admiral Jellicoe, said Churchill, was the only man who could have lost the war in a single afternoon – no wonder his tactics at the Battle of Jutland were cautious in the extreme.

The battle began just before 4.00 p.m. on 31 May when the two battle cruiser squadrons sighted each other off Jutland. As planned, Hipper immediately wheeled around and set off, at pace, back to the security of the guns promised by the High Seas Fleet. Beatty followed.

From the beginning, British gunnery was markedly inferior to that of the Germans and with the first shots fired when the battle cruiser squadrons were still eight miles apart it soon became apparent that Beatty was in trouble. Two of his ships, the *Indefatigable* and the *Queen Mary*, blew up and sank, lost with virtually all hands, while his own flagship, *Lion*, along with the *Tiger* and *Princess Royal*, were seriously damaged. It led Beatty to turn to his Flag Captain and utter his classic line, 'There seems to be something wrong with our bloody ships today.' [25]

Indeed there was. Quite apart from their poor gunnery, it was common practise in the Royal Navy to leave open the doors to the ammunition hoists when in action. Shells and cordite were stacked in open companionways to facilitate quicker firing. All of this was fine but when hit by shells it could lead to flash explosions which could – and did – destroy a ship in seconds. It was not all one way traffic, with Beatty managing to sink the *Von der Tann* and cripple three other battle cruisers, including the *Seydlitz* and *Lutzow*.

As dusk fell the two main battle fleets finally came within range of each other. As the British battleships opened fire Scheer suddenly realised his danger and turned away but not before sinking another battle cruiser, the *Invincible*. Jellicoe, only too aware of submarines and mines, also withdrew and headed back to port. Small actions between cruisers, destroyers and torpedo boats continued during the night, one German cruiser being sunk, but the main battle was over in less than five hours.

The question has often been asked, who won the Battle of Jutland? Certainly the British lost more ships – three battle cruisers, three cruisers and eight destroyers. In contrast the Germans lost one battleship, one battle cruiser, four cruisers and five destroyers.

But strategically Jutland was a clear British victory. Scheer knew how close he had come to disaster and the High Seas Fleet never again ventured out in anger. Britain still ruled the waves and clearly Germany did not. As a consequence, the British blockade of Germany was tightened, a tactic that ultimately led to Allied victory in the war.

Shells burst alongside the British battle cruisers.

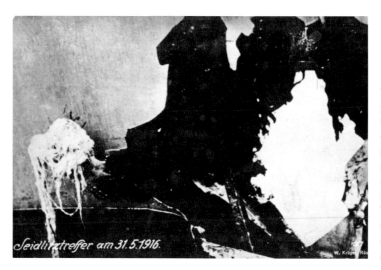

Vice Admiral Beatty might have asked 'What's wrong with our bloody ships today?' but he did inflict serious damage on some of the enemy vessels. This shows damage to the armour plating of the German *Seydlitz*.

Shells dropping close to the Grand Fleet.

The Submarine Threat

One of the major consequences of the Battle of Jutland was the Germans' final realisation that they could not defeat Britain at sea, at least not using traditional capital ships. They knew that if ever another Jutland was in the offing there could only ever be one winner.

With Hindenburg and Ludendorff advocating 'total war' the decision was made to reintroduce unrestricted submarine warfare. The order was given to stop ship yards from the building of battleships and cruisers. They were to concentrate, instead, on producing submarines.

Sailors were taken from the High Seas Fleet to be trained as submariners and before the year was out the U Boat threat had become very real indeed. With the Dover Straits closed to them, U Boats slipped silently out of Kiel and other German ports and proceeded on the long route around the north of Scotland. Once out in the Atlantic they lay waiting in the Western Approaches or off the coast of Ireland, watching for any unwary cargo ships.

The effect of the U Boat campaign was phenomenal. The average total of Allied merchant ships lost to submarines during 1916 rose dramatically from less than 90,000 tons a month to 190,000, a total that threatened to grow and overwhelm the always fragile infrastructure of any island nation.

There was, even at this early stage, one way to defeat the U Boat menace – convoys. Yet the Admiralty was strangely reluctant to introduce the system, believing that it would simply give the submarines a greater number of targets to aim at. And so, for the time being, cargo vessels were left to plough their lonely furrows across the world's oceans, trusting to luck and good judgement.

Lord Kitchener died on 5 June 1916, just a week after the Battle of Jutland. He was on his way to meet with members of the Russian government, hoping to renew their enthusiasm for the war, when his ship, HMS *Hampshire*, struck a mine and sank off the Orkneys. The mine was one of many laid by a German U Boat across the possible path of the Grand Fleet as it came out to fight Scheer and Hipper. Only fourteen men managed to reach safety and Kitchener was not one of them. He had been seen walking on deck, encouraging others, just before the ship went down, obviously resigned to his fate.

Bairnsfather's take on the submarine menace.

Lord Kitchener died in 1916, victim of a mine dropped by a German U Boat. The mine was intended to destroy one of Britain's battleships on its way to Jutland. Instead, it sank the cruiser *Hampshire* which was taking Kitchener to a meeting in Russia.

The End of the Zeppelin Scourge

Zeppelins had been harassing Britain since 1915 but their reign of terror was to be short-lived. Early in 1916, a force of nine airships raided towns in the Midlands but on the return trip one came down in the North Sea – Zeppelin pilots had been instructed to crash in the sea rather than on land as this would simply expose the secrets of the terror weapon to the British. All the crew from this crashed airship were drowned and took their secrets with them to the bottom of the sea. On 1 April, a Zeppelin engaged in bombing London was actually shot down by anti-aircraft fire, a rare early example of success against the airships.

The year 1916 saw the rise of the 'super zeppelin', 350 feet long and capable of flying well above the height most fighters could ever contemplate. These huge machines could carry five tons of bombs and were armed with ten machine guns. Despite this seeming invincibility, many of the new Zeppelins regularly failed to deal with severe wind conditions over the North Sea.

Then, in September, Lieutenant Leefe Robinson became the first pilot to shoot down a Zeppelin over British soil. He was not the first man to destroy a Zeppelin. This honour fell to Sub-Lieutenant R. A. J. Warneford, who brought down a Zeppelin between Ghent and Bruges on 7 June 1915. Warneford dropped six bombs onto the top of the Zeppelin which exploded in flames and crashed onto a Belgian convent. All of the crew and two nuns were killed. His VC for the attack was awarded posthumously as Warneford was killed in a flying accident ten days later.

Leefe Robinson, however, was the first man to shoot down a Zeppelin, using machine gun bullets rather than bombs. It was also the first night victory for a British fighter. Robinson spotted his victim over Essex, managed to climb above it and dive onto the unprotected top of the airship. He emptied two drums of ammunition into the Zeppelin which almost immediately caught fire and crashed in flames. For his bravery Leefe Robinson was awarded the Victoria Cross. [26]

In October 1916, Kapitan Heinrich Mathy, the most famous of all Zeppelin commanders, was killed when his ship, the L 31, was shot down by Lieutenant W. J. Tempest over Potters Bar. Tempest, like Leefe Robinson before him, was almost incinerated when the burning Zeppelin fell towards his plane.

Zeppelin commanders were ordered to ditch their craft in the sea, rather than come down on land as this might reveal their secrets to the British.

Above left: A Zeppelin caught in the searchlights of a British anti-aircraft battery. Illuminating them was one thing; shooting them down was another.

Above right: Lieutenant William Leefe Robinson, the first man to shoot down a Zeppelin over Britain. He was awarded the Victoria Cross for his actions but was later shot down by the Red Baron, Manfred von Richtofen, and spent the rest of the war as a prisoner.

The greatest disaster to befall the Zeppelins came just a few days later, on the night of 20 October. Eleven Zeppelins set off to attack Britain and, as they approached the English coast, ran into a full scale gale. One was blown across the French coast where it was destroyed by anti-aircraft fire. Another, after dropping a bomb on Piccadilly Circus, was also blown over France where she crashed and burned. Two others were blown right across France, one disappearing for ever over the Mediterranean, the other making a forced landing where she was captured intact. [27]

More than anything, the elements conspired in the defeat of the Zeppelins. Twenty-two raids had been launched against Britain in 1916, with limited degrees of success and huge losses to the Zeppelin fleet. After the disaster of October 1916 the raids were suspended and although long range bombers soon took their place they never quite had the power or the mystique to instil fear into the British people in the way that the Zeppelins had once done.

Casualty Stations

A clear system of aid to wounded soldiers had been established early in the war. Each Regiment had its own Medical Officer and, in general, these were the men who dealt with day to day medical problems through things like the traditional army sick call.

Wounded men were, if possible, dealt with on the spot, fellow soldiers applying bandages or first aid until the MO could see them. Orders were firm, however – nobody was to stop his advance to tend to the wounded. If a man was too seriously injured to remain at his post he would be taken – walking, if possible, carried by stretcher bearers if not – to the regimental aid post just behind the lines.

If the wound was serious enough to warrant it a man would then be moved to an advance dressing station, a little further back from the front line; behind that, again, came the clearing station. If a wounded man reached this point he had obviously received a 'Blighty Wound', an injury serious enough to have him sent home to Blighty. Transport to Base Hospital would follow, usually by train. Hospital trains in the early part of the war were well-equipped, often supplied by voluntary agencies. But as casualty figures mounted, stretchers were simply laid on the floor of the carriages or wagons and the wounded men had to cope as best they could.

Base Hospitals were situated on the coast, around towns like Boulogne, and here men would encounter not just doctors but nurses of the Queen Alexandra's Imperial Nursing Service. From here wounded men were shipped back to Britain. It was a blessed relief to be out of the fighting, but for many the respite was only temporary. All too soon they would be back at the front, risking life and limb once more.

Christmas in the Trenches

The Christmas Truce of 1914 was never repeated but the Christmas period was the one time of the year when soldiers on both sides of No Man's Land looked forward to a few moments of peace and extra comfort. The front lines still needed to be held but, unless Brigade was more than usually warlike, there was often little activity in the

Above left: Walking wounded; the first stage in getting injured men away from the front line.

Above right: Hospital trains took the wounded to Base Hospital – very rarely were they as comfortable or as clean as this Ambulance Train provided in 1914 by the Caledonian Railway Company. But then, in the early days nobody knew how many casualties there would be.

Wounded soldiers in their distinctive blue jackets. This group is shown attending a garden party at Stanton Drew.

Above left: Christmas greetings from the front – a silk or embroidered postcard. These were favourites of the British soldiers and were produced in great numbers by women, sometimes in their front parlours; real cottage industry.

Above right: A German Christmas card showing that the luxuries of home were still available to men at the front.

No matter how bad the war was going, Father Christmas would always be there, at least for these imaginary German soldiers.

Above left: The British were a little more philosophical in their approach to Christmas. This soldier from the 7th Division has a far away and wistful expression on his face. As can be seen from the battle honours the 7th Division has already notched up an impressive array of battles and campaigns.

Above right: Even prisoners of war produced and sent Christmas cards to their families. This example is from prisoners at Hann Munden.

General Joffre visits the front line.

trenches at this time. Christmas dinner – even if conditions forced it to be taken a day or so late – meant good food, beef and plum pudding instead of the usual stew. It was something to be looked forward to with relish.

As Christmas time approached, newspapers and magazines carried advertisements for Christmas gifts, things that would make life more bearable for the men in the trenches. These gifts ranged from fountain pens and pipes to foot warmers and mittens. Parcels from home certainly did make a difference on men's morale but it was usually items like cake and sweets that made the greatest impression.

Christmas cards and postcards were produced by UK publishers, usually with a humorous but pointed message – it might be Christmas but there was still a war to be won. German postcards tended to be far more traditional, emphasising humanity and good will to all (though not, of course, to the enemy).

Many Regiments produced their own Christmas cards. These were sent by the soldiers to loved ones at home and the cards often showed the battle honours of the particular Regiment. Even prisoners of war produced their own Christmas cards and, amazingly, these were sent and received by families at home. [28]

Changes at the Top

As 1916 ground to a close changes were afoot in several different spheres. That October, General Nivelle, one of the heroes of Verdun, had become a national hero when he retook much of the territory that had been lost to Germany in the earlier battle. Nivelle claimed that he had found the secret of victory and, although he resolutely refused to disclose quite what the secret was, the French people were desperate enough to clutch at any straw, however slight or fallible it might be.

'Pappa' Joffre was promoted to Marshal of France and, as delicately as possible, was 'pushed upstairs'. He had had a good innings but had failed to win the war. Now it was someone else's turn. Nivelle succeeded him as supreme commander on the Western Front.

In Britain there was much speculation and comment about the conduct of the war which, everyone agreed, was not going well. Lloyd George, always an inveterate conspirator, was at the heart of the debate and he was supported by the Conservative leader Andrew Bonar Law. That November, in something of a Palace Coup, they suggested that Asquith might like to remain as Prime Minister but that conduct of the war should rest in the hands of none other than Lloyd George. Asquith, after first seeming to agree, soon changed his mind and broke up the coalition government. His plan was to reform his cabinet without Lloyd George.

As a political move it was a disaster. Most MPs also wanted a more energetic and dynamic running of the war and, having seemingly got rid of H. H. Asquith, they were not going to let him back in. Lloyd George was their man. With support from both Liberals and Conservatives he duly became Prime Minister on 7 December 1916. Asquith retired into Opposition, the first formal Opposition since the coalition government had been formed in 1915.

Lloyd George immediately set up a War Cabinet of just five men – Bonar Law, Lords Curzon and Milner, and Arthur Henderson; and, of course, Lloyd George himself. It

Above left: At the end of 1916 Lloyd George replaced Asquith as Prime Minister after a period of intense wrangling and political in-fighting. It was, effectively, the end of Asquith's political career.

Above right: Bruce Bairnsfather's view of the thinking soldier, the man fighting for a better world.

was a small, powerful cabal, one that had the intelligence and the determination to take unpleasant but necessary decisions should the situation require it. They were men who had no other departmental duties, men who could concentrate on winning the war. If necessary they would bring in business men and Trade Unionists to advise and help. It had been a long, hard road but at last Britain had got the leadership she deserved. It was a leadership that might just win the war.

A Better World

As 1916 drew to a close it was obvious that Verdun and the Somme had destroyed the idealism of most soldiers. They had gone naively to the war, believing that they were helping Belgium, sure that the Kaiser and his plans for European, even world, domination had to be stopped. They had had no doubt about where right lay. Now they were faced by a new reality.

The war had not ended by Christmas, not even Christmas 1916. It would drag on, men thought, for ever, perhaps until they were all killed. The reasons why they had gone so blithely to war faded into the background, subsumed by the simple and basic need to survive. If I can just get through, they said, then things will be different.

It was from this time that the idea of creating a better world for soldiers to return to began to grow and flourish. All the other reasons for fighting counted as nothing in the face of that desire for a better world. That was all the men in the trenches could cling to, the idea of a better world.

1917 – Mud and Blood

The Hindenburg Line

Having taken command of the German forces in the west Hindenburg and Ludendorff quickly realised there was a need to shorten their line of trenches. This would make better use of manpower, fewer soldiers being required to defend the shorter front. So, during the winter of 1916/17, Russian POW's were set to work digging and building a new set of trenches, several miles behind the original ones, cutting across the base of a salient that had previously bulged out into Allied territory. When it was complete the new line, known by the British as the Hindenburg Line, shortened the German front line by almost thirty-five miles.

The Germans gave each section of the new line a name – the Siegfried Stellung, Alberial Stellung, Brunhilde Stellung and Kriemhilde Stellung. Of these the Siegfried Stellung, running from Arras to St Quentin, was considered impregnable. Events later in the year and again in the summer of 1918 proved that this was decidedly not the case but, even so, the new trench system was certainly impressive.

The German trench layouts had always been vastly superior to those of the Allies. They had come intending to stay while the British and French invariably saw their trenches as temporary affairs that would be abandoned once the Germans had been pushed out of France and Belgium. The Hindenburg Line, therefore, consisted of purpose built trenches, amazing pieces of military architecture that were designed to house soldiers, equipment and supplies, for years if necessary.

Concrete bunkers and deep tunnels to facilitate the movement of troops between one spot on the line and another were just part of the system. There were also concrete machine gun emplacements with wide arcs of fire and roll upon roll of barbed wire. In front of the line were fortified Outpost Villages, carefully designed to give covering fire to each other and guaranteed to hold up any attack until reinforcements arrived.

In February 1917, the German Army began to withdraw to these carefully prepared lines. The land between the old front and the new one was deliberately obliterated, a scorched earth policy that left just open fields of mud that any attacking force would now have to cross.

Painting and Poetry

As early as August 1914 the British government realised that the country was lagging far behind Germany as far as propaganda was concerned. As a result the British War Propaganda Bureau was formed under Charles Masterman and over the next eighteen

British soldiers sit in captured German trenches.

Above left: Louis Raemaekers' cartoons of the German advance into Belgium were the source of much debate and proved to be the inspiration for Official British War Artists.

Above right: German prisoners at the roadside, a drawing by Sir William Orpen, one of many War Artists.

months a steady stream of books and booklets was produced by people like John Buchan, Thomas Hardy and Rudyard Kipling, all emphasising the righteousness and success of the war.

When the Bureau published a report into the German atrocities in Belgium they illustrated it with the work of Dutch artist Louis Raemaekers. His graphic depictions of the 'rapacious Hun' brought a stunning response from the public and Masterman suddenly realised the value of art as a propaganda tool. He decided to send professional artists out to France to depict life in the trenches.

The remit was clear, however. There were to be no dead bodies, no wounded men and Germans, if shown at all, had to be prisoners of the British. Despite such crippling restrictions War Artists still managed to produce quality work that really did capture the horror and the essence of what war was really like. The format was quite simple. An artist would go to the front where he would stay for several weeks, and then retire to the rear areas where he could turn his sketches into paintings. After a month or two the artist would be replaced by another painter or cartoonist – and so on.

Muirhead Bone was the first Official War Artist but over the next few years he was joined by over ninety fellow artists. Some of them, like Paul Nash, Sir William Orpen, Frank Brangwyn and C. R. W. Nevinson produced stunning paintings and drawings that, even now, still stand the test of time. Others, like Augustus John, produced virtually nothing. Many of their paintings, defying the restraints imposed by Masterman, were so realistic that they were only able to be shown after the war. Restrictions did relax somewhat once Lord Beaverbrook took over as Minister for Information in 1918 but the conflict between reality and propaganda remained in place right to the end. [29]

From the beginning of the war, poets had tried to put their thoughts and feelings about the conflict into words. It began with the patriotic verses of men like Rupert Brooke and Julian Grenfell and ended with the vitriol and realism of Siegfried Sassoon and Wilfred Owen. The early writings of Brooke, in particular, have been heavily criticised but they have to be put into the context of the time. Brooke might well write:

Frank Brangwyn's view of the war was dark and dangerous – small wonder many of his most powerful drawings were not published until the war ended.

A Painting by
C. R. W. Nevinson,
a War Artist and
friend of the poet
Isaac Rosenberg.
This view of No
Man's Land after a
battle is, you feel, an
accurate depiction.

> If I should die, think only this of me:
> That there's some corner of a foreign field
> That is for ever England. (30)

But in 1914 that was exactly how people were thinking. And there is no doubt that, had he survived the Gallipoli Campaign, Rupert Brooke would have produced some of the finest and most realistic poetry of the whole war.

By the end of 1916 and the beginning of 1917, things had changed. Sassoon was now seriously critical of the way the war was being run, sure that it was being prolonged just so that capitalists could make more money. He even threw his Military Cross into the Mersey in protest. And his poems are full of caustic, satirical comment that shocked both the High Command and society in general:

> Does it matter? – losing your legs? ...
> For people will always be kind,
> And you need not show that you mind
> When the others come in after hunting
> To gobble their muffins and eggs. [31]

Wilfred Owen was far less satirical than Sassoon but his realism and depictions of life at the front stay with the reader long after the poems have been put aside. His, surely, is the voice of the ordinary man caught up in a conflict that he can neither understand nor explain. He can only describe what he sees:

> What passing bells for those who die as cattle?
> Only the monstrous anger of the guns.
> Only the stuttering rifles' rapid rattle
> Can patter out their hasty orisons. [32]

".. ABOVE ALL I AM NOT CONCERNED WITH POETRY.
MY SUBJECT IS WAR, AND THE PITY OF WAR.
THE POETRY IS IN THE PITY.."

Wilfred Owen – 'My subject is war and the pity of war.' Owen, perhaps the greatest poet to emerge from the Great War, died just a few days before it ended. The victory bells were pealing in his home town of Shrewsbury when his parents received the news of his death.

Unlike the Official War Artists, the poets of the Great War were serving soldiers whose primary aim or concern was to defeat the enemy. Many of them died, including Owen, Edward Thomas, Isaac Rosenberg and the Welsh language poet Hedd Wyn, (real name Ellis Evans) whose Eisteddfod Chair was awarded posthumously in 1917.

Trying to make sense out of the horror of the trenches and No Man's Land was something all artists, whatever their genre or form, tried to do. They were lucky; they had the means and the skill to do it. For most of the soldiers of the Great War there was nothing to do but grin and bear it, to bury their heads and pray for the war to finally end.

Revolution in Russia

By the beginning of 1917 it was clear that the Russians were in dire straits. The Czar had always ruled as a despot – despite the nominal existence of the Duma or people's Parliament – and from September 1915 he had taken personal charge of the running of the war. He was often away from home, at the front, directing operations that should have been left to his generals – and not directing them particularly well.

That left his wife, Czarina Alexandra, to take charge of domestic affairs at the Russian court. Heavily influenced by the mystic and mysterious monk, Gregory Rasputin, who seemed to have the power to help and heal her haemophilic son, Alexandra made several stupid blunders, dismissing influential court officials who could and should have been offering realistic advice. Being of German origin, there was a great dislike of Alexandra in the country and when the ordinary man or woman in the street looked at the corruption and opulence of the Czar's court they could be excused for asking who was making all the sacrifices in the war.

During the winter of 1916/17 there were serious food shortages in all of the Russian cities. Casualty lists were enormous and the war seemed no closer to a conclusion. In early March, strikes and serious food riots broke out in Petrograd and a regiment of soldiers, desperate to avoid being sent to the front, quickly joined the protesters. When a regiment of Cossacks was ordered to fire on the rioters they refused. Mobs charged along the streets and broke into the prisons, releasing many of the political prisoners who had been held in captivity. The Duma now voiced open criticism of the Czar and, ignoring his orders, refused to disband.

Czar Nicholas, finally realising there was chaos in the capital, attempted to leave the front and return to Petrograd. Railway workers stopped his train and forced him back to military headquarters at the front. Faced by seething revolution from the people, the soldiers among them, his generals advised abdication. Reluctantly, Nicholas agreed. The Romanov dynasty that had ruled Russia for hundreds of years had collapsed and disappeared in a matter of weeks.

A new liberal and democratic government was set up, headed by the lawyer Alexander Kerensky. Even then, ominous stirrings could be seen in the shape of Socialist peoples groups known as Soviets that, in the wake of the Czar's departure, had been established. Slowly and carefully, they increased their power over the things that mattered to the population – food, fuel and effective local government. At this stage Kerensky was clear; there was no intention of leaving the war. The Czar was blamed for the bad running of the country and its war effort. His liberal government would do better.

The German leadership soon realised that Kerensky intended to honour Russia's pledge to fight alongside France and Britain. The revolutionary Lenin, leader of Russia's Bolshevik faction, had been forced to leave the country many years before and was then living in exile in Switzerland. As a Marxist, his long-stated aim was to overthrow all national governments and create a system of international Socialism but, importantly, he also believed that if Russia withdrew from the conflict other warring nations would soon follow its lead.

Ludendorff seized on Lenin's words and provided him with a sealed train to travel through Germany into Russia. He also gave Lenin money to help with the second revolution that he hoped would occur now that the Bolshevik leader was back in Russia. True to his word, Lenin arrived in Petrograd on 16 April 1917 and within a few days had denounced the new Provisional Government. There, joined by Leon Trotsky, he began preaching revolution.

America Enters the War

In line with the concept of 'total war' Germany announced the introduction of unrestricted submarine warfare at the end of January 1917. From now on, all shipping – Allied or neutral – would be sunk on sight if it was found in the eastern Atlantic. Hindenburg and Ludendorff believed the policy, effectively starving Britain to death, would bring them victory within six months. In reality it was one of the major factors that brought the USA into the war and, eventually, spelled German defeat.

The idea of unrestricted submarine warfare was abhorrent to the Americans, not so much because of the loss of innocent life but because so many American ships, loaded with valuable goods, would now either be sunk or, fearing what might await them in

The sheer opulence of the Winter Palace in Petrograd caused much resentment in the Russian people.

Above left: With people starving all over Russia it was no surprise that the Bolsheviks highlighted the decadence of the Romanov dynasty. Such finery, they declared, would feed a hundred families for a hundred years.

Above right: With the Czar away at the front it was left to his wife to run the domestic affairs of the Empire. And Alexandra was as inefficient at that as Nicholas was at running the war.

the Atlantic, remain tied up in port. Either way, there was likely to be a huge loss of revenue for American businessmen.

Since the start of war huge quantities of wheat, cotton and raw materials for industry had been streaming across the Atlantic. It was not just the capitalist businessmen who had made themselves fortunes. Wages were high, factories worked overtime – it was certainly a time of plenty for all Americans. Now all this looked like it could go. The very people who had been lobbying the President, Congress and Senate to stay out of the war now began to change their tune. The spectre of war inched decidedly closer.

The immediate cause of the USA joining the war, however, was the Zimmerman Telegram. On 16 January, knowing what was to come in the weeks ahead, the German Foreign Secretary, Arthur Zimmerman, sent a blatantly ill-advised and dangerous telegram to the Mexican government. In it he proposed that in return for Mexico joining Germany in an alliance, there would be huge rewards. Once the Great War was won, Germany would help Mexico to regain, Zimmerman said, Texas, New Mexico and Arizona. It was a fatuous offer. There was no way Germany could ever back up such an offer and, anyway, the Mexicans had no desire to declare war on the USA.

There have been subsequent claims that the telegram was fake. It was, many believe, simply a ploy by British intelligence to bring the USA into the war. It seems, now, that the telegram was genuine and, short sighted as it might seem, Zimmerman really did hope to drag Mexico into the war.

The telegram was intercepted, decoded by the British government and, eventually, the full text was printed in the American newspapers. It was enough, all that President Woodrow Wilson needed. On 6 April 1917, the USA declared war on Germany. It would be several months before America could put an army into the field, the first 14,000 doughboys arriving in France that August. And they would have to undergo intensive training before they would be ready for the trenches. But Germany's worst fear had been realised, America had joined the Allies.

The Battle of Arras

In an attempt to distract German attention from French preparations for an assault, sometimes called the Nivelle Offensive, Field Marshal Haig had allowed himself to be persuaded that it was time for British troops to attack again. This time the area chosen was at Arras.

The Battle of Arras began on 9 April with the now customary bombardment. And to begin with there was considerable success. The Canadians of the First Army took Vimy Ridge, capturing many guns and prisoners in the process. And then, after an advance of five miles, the attack ground to a halt in front of the Hindenburg Line. This was where the Battle of Arras should have ended. After all, it had achieved its aim and diverted the Germans from Nivelle's preparations. But, of course, the thought of the final dramatic breakthrough was too great for a cavalryman like Haig.

On 23 April, the attacks began again and this time, with no element of surprise, they achieved nothing. The Germans had brought up reserves and were ready. The Battle of Arras cost Britain 150,000 casualties, among them the poet Edward Thomas who was

With Russia clearly on her last legs the Allies were much relieved when, in April 1917, the USA entered the war on their side. The doughboys would, as their song suggested, be 'over there!'

Above left: General Pershing, commander of the American Armies, with Foch, soon to be supreme commander of all Allied Armies.

Above right: Holding on until the end – by 1917 it was all most soldiers could do.

killed by the blast of an artillery shell in the opening moments of the battle. German casualties amounted to 100,000.

The Nivelle Offensive

General Nivelle, the man who had claimed to hold the secret to winning the war, launched his offensive on the River Aisne on 16 April. Nivelle might well have had the secret but his plan of campaign was already known to the Germans. A French NCO had been captured with full details of the attack in his coat pocket – although quite why a lowly NCO should have such details about his person has never been properly explained.

The early stages of the battle had been marred for the French by the German 'scorched earth' policy and the land the soldiers had to cross was a quagmire of mud and booby traps. As ever, the preliminary bombardment was ineffective, failing to break the wire and serving only to churn up the ground even more. The Germans were sheltering deep under ground until the bombardment ended and then, when the French soldiers advanced, they walked into a hail of machine gun fire. Despite Haig's diversionary battle to the north, the Germans had moved extra troops to the area and were more than ready for the French assault.

It was yet another blood bath. The French lost 96,000 men and instead of gaining six miles, as Nivelle had boasted, the gain was a paltry six hundred yards. Nivelle had promised that the battle would be over in two days. In the event it lasted two weeks and then simply faded into the normal routine of trench warfare.

For Nivelle the failure was decisive. At the end of the month, before the final echoes of his great offensive had even died away, he was replaced by Henri Petain, the hero of Verdun, who was unceremoniously hauled out of retirement. Nivelle's time had gone but, significantly, his legacy to the French Army was something far worse than death in battle. It was mutiny.

A dead soldier; the real pity of war.

The French Army Mutinies

Nivelle's Offensive had been the final straw for the demoralised and battered French soldiers. Verdun had virtually crippled them; the Nivelle Offensive took them to breaking point.

The mutiny was not an ordered response, rather it was something that occurred and then spread. All along the French front soldiers simply lay down their arms and refused to fight. In all, fifty-four Divisions took up the stance and even those that did not join in marched towards the lines bleating like sheep. They were only too aware of what awaited them but were too exhausted and shell shocked to do anything more about it than voice their disapproval in this way.

For some who went up at this perilous time, it wasn't bleating like sheep that voiced their feelings. Some of them sang what has now become known as 'The Song of Despair':

> Goodbye life, goodbye love, goodbye all women.
> It is well finished, it is for always,
> This infamous war.
> It is in Caonne, on the plate,
> That one must leave his skin
> Because we are all condemned,
> We are sacrificed.
> (Anon) 33

By some strange and unexplained miracle the Germans did not know about the mutinies, did not realise that miles of the French front lines were left undefended. Perhaps they, too, were exhausted. Nivelle's Offensive had cost them over 80,000 dead or captured and it is possible that they were content to sit and lick their wounds. For whatever reason they did not know, which was just as well. Had they realised they could have simply walked through the French lines and been in Paris within a few days.

Petain, the new French commander, acted swiftly but ruthlessly to stop the mutinies. Over 90,000 French soldiers were court martialled, 23,000 being found guilty for their part in the affair. Originally, 432 were sentenced to death but clemency was now the order of the day and, eventually, no more than 55 of the main leaders were actually shot. Rumours still abound of many more mutineers being shelled to death by the French artillery.

The mutinies stopped fairly quickly and Petain guaranteed to look at issues such as extra rations and a decent leave allowance for all soldiers. Yet the situation remained delicate. Petain, and the other Allied leaders, knew that the French Army would not regain its position as an effective fighting force for many months. For some time to come the weight of continuing the war would rest on the shoulders of Douglas Haig and the British Army.

The U Boat Threat

By the early summer of 1917 the U Boats were tightening their grip around the British coast. That April alone more than a million tons of Allied and neutral shipping were sent to the bottom and almost one vessel in four that left port bound for Britain never returned home. These were losses that were impossible to sustain and, with Britain dependent on imported food stuff, there was a very real threat that starvation and lack of raw materials for the war effort might defeat the country where Ludendorff and the whole German Army had failed. Soon American ships were refusing to sail if their destination was any British port.

The main U Boat bases were in Ostend and Zeebrugge and from here the submarines were able to slip out to take their positions in the Western Approaches. David Lloyd George knew that the answer was the introduction of the convoy system but the so-called experts at Admiralty were equally as convinced that it would not work.

Merchant ships would never be able to keep the rigid formation demanded by a convoy, the Admiralty argued. And besides, there were not enough destroyers and escort vessels to set up a suitable screen. Lloyd George knew differently. He prepared his case thoroughly, gathering facts and figures about the number of ships entering British ports and the availability of escort vessels. And when he was ready, he struck.

At a meeting in the Admiralty on 26 April he simply overrode all arguments and, as Prime Minister, ordered that a system of convoys be put in place. The men of the Admiralty quickly and easily gave in. The first convoy sailed on 10 May and in the weeks ahead it was seen to be a clear success. Sinkings dropped dramatically and, as the destroyer crews became used to working the depth charges, the toll of U Boats destroyed began to rise. Soon Britain was sinking submarines far faster than the German dockyards could build them.

The use of Q Ships also added to the toll of enemy submarines destroyed. These were decoy vessels, small ships that appeared to be too inconsequential to waste a torpedo on. Yet when the U Boat surfaced to destroy the ship by gunfire, hidden guns on the deck of the tramp steamer or coaster were revealed and the German crew quickly realised that they had bitten off more than they could chew. The earliest Q Ships were in use by late 1914 but they really came into their own in 1916 and 1917.

Convoys were not universally employed. In the Mediterranean, for example, and around the coast of Britain they were simply not used at all. And in these areas the U Boats continued to reap a grim harvest. In the end it was a close run thing – at one stage there was less than a month's supply of wheat in the whole country – but by the end of the year it was clear that the convoy system was working. The U Boat threat had been nullified and in the months ahead it would be utterly destroyed.

War in the Air

The value of aircraft as offensive weapons – as opposed to their original use as simple reconnaissance vehicles – grew slowly but firmly as the war went on. When Max Immelmann flew over Paris in August 1914, dropping a note informing the inhabitants

A mock execution, although quite why it should be taking place is not known. Over 300 British soldiers were shot by their own side during the war, most of them for desertion in the face of the enemy. After the French mutinies of 1917 fifty-five French soldiers were shot as an example to others.

A captured U Boat, towed into British port.

Depth charges explode over a hunted U Boat. The combination of convoys and improved anti-submarine tactics did eventually win the battle for the British.

A convoy proceeds
steadily out to sea.

that the German Army was at the gates, it set a precedent – soon both sides would be
dropping things far more lethal from their aeroplanes.

It quickly became standard practise for aircraft to make bombing attacks on targets
close to the front – railway stations, armaments depots and so on. These were not
always particularly successful and were certainly not coordinated in any way. However,
by 1917 British High Command had realised the advantages of a strategic bombing
campaign and formed the Independent Air Force with a view to bombing certain
strategic targets far beyond the lines. Marshalling yards and armament factories were
obvious targets and cities such as Cologne and Dusseldorf were now well within range
of the new British bombers.

The real glamour, however, came in the shape of the fighter pilots. These young men,
who had a life expectancy of just weeks, flew their flimsy craft high over the trenches
in an effort to shoot down enemy fighters and bombers. The Royal Flying Corps
maintained a policy of offensive action right through the war, regardless of casualties,
and this meant that many, if not most, of their engagements took place over enemy
territory. With the prevailing wind from the west it also meant that pilots faced a long
and arduous flight home after the combat was over.

Germany and France had long rejoiced in their 'aces', pilots who had scored more
than five aerial victories. Frenchmen like Charles Nungesser and Georges Guynemer
were household names while, in Germany, aces like Boelcke and Immelmann had,
after their deaths in combat, been superseded by men such as Werner Voss and Bruno
Loerzer. Above all, there was the remote but deadly Manfred von Richtofen, the famous
Red Baron.

Richtofen was not a natural pilot but he was a natural killer, a hunter who loved to
destroy – and it didn't matter if the target was wild boar or British fighter pilots. He
eventually claimed eighty Allied aircraft before he was, in turn, shot down in 1918.
The credit for downing the Red Baron was initially given to the Canadian Roy Brown
but it was more likely to be machine gun fire from the ground that eventually ended
the career of Manfred von Richtofen.

Britain was slow to acknowledge its aces, believing it was wrong to single out a few
individuals when the whole of the RFC was performing gallantly on a daily basis. It was
only in the middle of 1917 when the rumours of deeds performed by a band of intrepid

Above left: British and French pilots line up for a presentation. The aircraft in the background are RE8s, a standard British reconnaissance plane throughout the war years.

Above right: Germany was always more adept at praising her flyers, as this postcard shows.

The air war took a terrible toll, on both sides – hardly surprising when pilots did not have parachutes and their planes were liable to catch fire whenever they were hit by machine gun bullets. This shows an RFC graveyard, complete with old propellers as headstones.

flyers on the Western Front, circulated by pilots home on leave, finally persuaded the government it should afford these daring young men some measure of publicity. Soon the names of Albert Ball, James McCudden and Mick Mannock had assumed an aura that grew to surround all flyers.

The story of fighter aircraft during the Great War is one of development and counter development as one nation came up with a new device or aeroplane only to see it superseded by some revolutionary new weapon from the other side. French pilot Roland Garros began it when he fitted metal blades to the propeller of his Morane Saulnier Scout, enabling him to fire forward through the propeller. Any bullets that hit the prop would bounce off the metal blades – which was fine, until one day he shot off his own propeller and was captured.

Garros and his piece of ingenuity were followed by Anthony Fokker's revolutionary interrupter device and the Fokker Eindekker. The British countered this with the DH2. Then came the Albatross fighter, matched by the Nieuport Scout and the Sopwith Pup. Germany soon produced the Fokker Triplane, Britain the Sopwith Camel and the SE5. And so it went on, until it culminated in the most perfect warplane of the war, the Sopwith Snipe. Fast, sleek and robust, the Snipe appeared in the skies over the Western Front in the late summer of 1918. Only 200 or so ever made it to France but it was the culmination of four years steady technological development.

The stresses and strains of flying fighters on the Western Front – without parachutes and in flimsy canvas coated aircraft that could erupt into a mass of flames at any moment – was immense. There was no recognition of things like shell shock and stress. Pilots had no alternative but to struggle on to the end, an end that Guynemer recorded as the final decoration, 'the wooden cross'.

Passchendaele (Third Ypres)

By the summer of 1917 it was obvious that the British Army would have to launch yet another assault. The French still needed time to recover from the mutinies earlier in the year and the Americans had not yet begun to arrive in force. There is also little doubt that Haig was keen to finish things before the Americans began to make their presence felt. He had always favoured an attack in Flanders and now he seized the chance.

Haig's plan for the Battle of Passchendaele, or Third Ypres as it is more correctly known, was ambitious. If he could take the village and ridge of Passchendaele, he felt, there would be nothing to stop him reaching Roulers, from where he could release his cavalry to take the Channel ports and maybe even penetrate deeply into Germany. He did not realise that the Hindenburg Line reached up into this part of Belgium and that key points like Pilkem Ridge were heavily defended.

The battle was, quite simply, one of the most horrendous and appalling ever fought. The offensive was due to begin on 23 July 1917 but was postponed for seven days to allow French artillery to be ready and the opening assaults did not take place until 31 July. They continued for another three months. Canadian troops finally entered Passchendaele village on 6 November and by then the battle had cost 250,000 British casualties. German losses were about the same and although Passchendaele itself had

A crashed German aeroplane and the ruins of a forest in France – an enigmatic and powerful photo.

Above left: The Sopwith Snipe, possibly the greatest aeroplane of the whole war. Tragically very few of them went into service.

Above right: The Battle of Passchendaele, British soldiers charging towards Pilkem Ridge.

Above left: Taking a breather for a few minutes, soldiers drop behind a bank to gather themselves for another push.

Above right: A classic view of Passchendaele, blasted trees and thick mud. When one British general saw the battlefield he was moved to cry, 'My God, did we really send men to fight in that?'

The battles between Austria and Italy continued with the death toll rising steadily. Fighting took place on mountains and in valleys, always fierce, always deadly.

been captured it was too late in the year to allow any reasonable exploitation of the success.

The horror of Passchendaele seems to sum up the suffering of the men in the trenches during the Great War. The opening artillery barrage of the battle had lasted for over a week, tons and tons of shells raining down on the German trenches and No Man's Land. The shelling had little effect on German defences but simply destroyed the drainage system of the area, breaching the canals and turning the whole front into a quagmire. To make matters worse, it began to rain on the first morning of the attack and did not seem to stop for months.

The name Passchendaele is now synonymous with mud and by the end of the first day the whole area was little more than a filthy morass of silt and slime. Men fell and drowned in the mud; they lived for weeks up to their knees in water. And yet this battle of attrition probably had a more damaging effect on the German Army than any other battle. From this point onwards they were simply hanging on, dead in the water. The trouble was, only men like Hindenburg and Ludendorff realised it.

The Caporetto Campaign

A series of drawn or inconclusive battles between Italy and Austria-Hungary had seemed to symbolise the campaigns in the Isonzo area, with the Italians constantly attempting to drive forward into the plains beyond the mountains and the Austrians always managing to push them back. When the Italian General Luigi Cadorna finally managed to achieve some success in the sector in the summer of 1917, it so alarmed Austria's ally Germany that Hindenburg and Ludendorff realised the Italian threat had to be eliminated for once and for all.

In October, a combined Austrian-German force crossed the Isonzo River and hurled itself at the Italians. The flanks of the Italian Army managed to hold but the centre, around Caporetto, quickly gave way. General Cadorna was replaced by General Diaz and reinforcements from Britain and France, desperate to keep Italy in the war, were rushed to the area. The Austro-German armies were eventually fought to a standstill but from Ludendorff's perspective it had been a successful campaign.

Over 200,000 Italians had been lost and, significantly, nearly half a million had deserted. Nearly 290,000 had been taken prisoner and would spend the rest of the war in prisoner of war camps.

There would be no more significant threats from Italy towards Austria-Hungary, even though British forces were now permanently encamped at Montello. But perhaps the most significant outcome of the whole campaign was the creation of a Supreme War Council. Lloyd George was clear – the recent campaigns on the Italian front showed that there needed to be a consistent and properly planned war policy between all the Allied nations. Men like Vittorio Orlando, Prime Minister of Italy, agreed with him. Consequently, the first War Council met at Versailles on 5 November. From now on there would be a united approach to the running of the war.

Above left: The Alpine soldier and the clean mountain air – it was never this perfect.

Above right: Motor transport improved greatly as the war progressed. Apart from a tendency to get stuck in the mud, lorries were a lot more reliable than horses.

Motor bikes were another great boon to the soldiers, particularly for delivering despatches and messages.

New Inventions – Motor Transport

It seems strange to think that in a war which saw the introduction of the fighter aeroplane, the development of tanks and the first concerted use of submarines the main form of transport was the horse. Despite the use of Paris taxis to get men to the Battle of the Marne, despite the famous London buses that took the BEF to the front in 1914, most transport remained horse drawn, right to the end of the conflict. Horses pulled the guns, horses dragged ammunition lumbers, and horses brought up rations and supplies.

However, as the war progressed there was a growing realisation that motor transport was the way things would go in the future. Horses needed to be fed and looked after. They could die or be seriously injured by enemy shelling. Motor transport consisted, after all, of just pieces of metal machinery.

Gradually, vans and lorries were introduced, being used to carry supplies and men. Motor bikes and armoured cars were issued to the troops, motor bikes in particular being very useful in the crowded lanes and streets of war-torn France. By the end of the war the more insightful observers were realising that, in the future, motorised transport was going to replace the horse.

New Inventions – Anti-Aircraft Guns

With the advent of the aeroplane and the Zeppelin it quickly became clear that new weapons required new forms of defence. And one of the best ways, it was decided, was artillery, artillery that fired shells into the air. In the early days there were limited anti-aircraft weapons in use in France but as the Zeppelin attacks on London and other cities mounted in ferocity, Sir Percy Scott was appointed to organise the defences of the British capital.

Batteries of guns and searchlights – even the guns of light cruisers moored in the Thames – were soon being employed. The AA guns, high angle Vickers 3 pounders, were mounted on lorries, being driven to wherever the danger was greatest.

At the front the Allies quickly realised the value of the French 75 mm artillery pieces, which could be elevated to a fairly high angle, and these were also soon mounted on lorries as mobile AA batteries. The Germans preferred a rapid fire 3.7 cm artillery piece, a weapon they used to great effect on the Somme, being deadly against low flying aircraft.

British pilots referred to anti-aircraft fire as Archie. The term apparently came from a popular song of the day – 'Archibald, Certainly Not!' – and can be traced back to a pilot of Number 4 Squadron RFC who would laugh derisively whenever he saw the bursting artillery shells and sing the ribald song at them. When his colleagues heard what he was doing, Archibald was duly shortened to Archie and remained the popular term for anti-aircraft fire until the end of the war. 34

Archie fire was always easily identified – British Archie burst with white smoke, German with black – even if it was not altogether successful. Many pilots claimed that Archie never hit anything. This was not quite true but small dots high up in the sky

CAMPAGNE DE 1914-1915

Visé Paris N° 535

Automobile blindée, tir contre Aéroplanes.

ND. Phot.

Anti-aircraft guns improved to keep pace with aircraft development.

were notoriously difficult to spot, let alone hit. Aircraft operating low down, closer to the ground, were much easier targets when machine guns could also be put to use. This was how both Richtofen and the British ace Mick Mannock eventually met their ends.

New Weapons – Tanks

Tanks were first introduced during the Battle of the Somme where Haig had hoped they might be available for the opening attack. Despite having the cavalry man's traditional scepticism about any offensive weapon other than a horse, he was at least willing to see how these new tanks performed.

The new wonder weapon was not ready for 1 July, however, and it was to be 15 September before the first forty-nine vehicles lumbered into action. Their appearance did not herald a glorious success. Nine broke down, a dozen more were too slow to keep up with the soldiers and several more quickly became bogged down in the mud of the battlefield.

The feeling was that if there had been more tanks available then they might have produced better results. As it was, there were too few of them, they were too slow and while they undoubtedly offered protection to the men inside their armoured hulls, they seemed to offer little help to the soldiers who still had to slog through the mud and filth outside. News of the new weapon quickly spread back home, however, and when tanks were used as a fund raising tool in the towns and cities of Britain during 1918 they attracted visitors in their thousands.

The name tank was an odd one to describe these lumbering great beasts with their metal tracks or treads. It came from the makers whose workmen believed they were making parts for water tanks. This was the name emblazoned on the sides of the crates and the name tank stuck.

The psychological effect of the appearance of the tanks was considerable. Initially at least, the German soldiers did not know what was coming at them. They stared in wonder and many of them certainly ran away. Such a reaction was short lived as they soon saw the tanks floundering in the mud or stuck on barbed wire. Nevertheless,

GUERRE AÉRIENNE – Canon employé par les Allemands pour tirer contre les aéroplanes
AERIAL WAR – Gun employed by the Germans for firing at the aeroplanes

Visé, Paris

German anti-aircraft shells exploded with clouds of black smoke, British with white. It certainly made it easier for pilots to see who was firing at them.

Tanks were introduced during the Battle of the Somme and again, with rather more success, at Cambrai. For the British public they were a source of fascination and when they were used to raise funds for the war effort – as in this 1917 photograph of a War Bond Rally in Pembroke Dock – they brought in hundreds of pounds.

A typical British tank and its crew.

there was obviously clear potential here and the appearance of three tanks in the main street was instrumental in the fall of Thiepval later that September. However, it was a little later in November that the new weapon really came into its own.

The Battle of Cambrai

The German High Command had seen how tanks performed at the Battle of the Somme. They were not impressed and considered them of little value. Some limited use in the mud of Passchendaele had simply confirmed their view.

So when, on 20 November 1917, the Germans were greeted by the sight of 380 tanks trundling across the fields before them they were more than startled. They were scared. This was the opening moment of the Battle of Cambrai. General Byng, the officer in command, had decided that there should be no preliminary bombardment of the enemy trenches. As far as he was concerned, the artillery should be saved for use after the initial objectives had been gained – let the tanks and the element of surprise do their work.

Initially the British attack was hugely successful. Disconcerted by the tanks the Germans abandoned their first line of trenches and fell back in disarray – the Hindenburg Line had been breached. And that was where things should have stopped. It was not to be. The cavalry was immediately ordered forward but machine gun fire from the second and third line of trenches halted them in their tracks. Low flying German aircraft were also used to strafe the advancing infantry and the attacks, as ever, simply ground to a halt.

At the end of the opening day 170 out of the 380 tanks employed that morning were out of action, either damaged by shellfire or left on the battlefield stuck in the mud. Despite their initial success the new tanks had not achieved anything like their potential and many began to doubt that they ever would. The Battle of Cambrai rumbled on for several weeks before finally ending on 5 December with 47,000 British casualties.

The November Revolution

Despite having unceremoniously 'ditched' the Czar, Kerensky's decision to continue the war was soon proved to be a foolhardy one. Russia suffered a serious defeat in July 1917 and German forces even managed to reach the outskirts of Riga. Despite the best efforts of Kerensky and his Provisional Government the Russians had lost all heart. The soldiers wanted simply to go home and they began to desert in droves.

Kerensky knew that the country's only hope was to sign a separate peace with Germany but his allies refused to even consider such a proposal. Kerensky, realising that further revolution was simmering, tried to come down hard. He arrested many Bolshevik leaders and Lenin fled to Finland. When the German forces took Riga that September, General Kornilov, the latest Commander-in-Chief, realising that the war was lost, promptly marched on Petrograd. If he could not defeat Germany, he could at least try to destroy the Revolution and, perhaps, restore the Czar to his throne.

A tank in action at the Battle of Cambrai. The tanks startled and frightened the Germans but did not achieve the breakthrough that had been hoped for. Far too many broke down or found themselves suck in the mud.

Above left: German dead in their trenches after a battle.

Above right: A Punch cartoon taking Bolshevik Russia to task for having the temerity to pull out of the war.

The situation was now reversed. Thoroughly alarmed, Kerensky armed the factory workers and released men like Trotsky from prison. He need not have bothered. Kornilov's soldiers made no attempt to capture Petrograd. They halted outside the city and either joined the Bolsheviks or simply headed off for home and safety. Trotsky and his Red Guards now had control of Petrograd and Kerensky and his government were clinging on by their fingertips.

For several weeks nothing seemed to happen. Lenin returned from Finland, Trotsky continued to make speeches. Then, in October, Kerensky struck. It was a massive misjudgement. He closed down the Bolshevik newspaper *Pravda* and in retaliation Trotsky seized the Post Office and the railway stations.

The cruiser *Aurora*, the main training ship of the Russian Baltic Fleet, was moored off the city. On the night of 25/26 October, sailors on board fired a shot at the Winter Palace, home to Kerensky's Provisional Government – it later transpired that it was a blank – as the signal for workers, soldiers and sailors to storm the palace. Kerensky hung on for a little while but, eventually realising his support had evaporated, he left the city and slipped out of the pages of history. Lenin assumed power – Communist Russia had arrived. He immediately made peace advances to Germany, advances that were eagerly accepted.

Germany might have been hugely successful in her campaigns against Russia but a war on two fronts had been costly in all respects and now here was the chance to end it. An Armistice was immediately signed, being converted into the hugely punitive Treaty of Brest-Litovsk in March the following year. Russia was out of the war.

Humour

It seems strange to think that in the wake of bloodbaths like the Somme and Passchendaele, men could still find both time and things to laugh at. And yet they did.

The November Revolution that brought Lenin and the Bolsheviks to power began when the cruiser *Aurora* fired a shot at the Winter Palace. It was the signal for a rising against Kerensky and his Provisional Government. The ship is now a museum in St Petersburg.

Humour was in evidence right through the war, sometimes self deprecating, sometimes harsh and satirical. Whatever its format it was always there – after all, faced by the horrors of the Ypres Salient or the flies of Dardanelles there was little else men could do but laugh at their predicament.

Humour was there in the soldiers' songs that they sang on the march or in the estaminet, often scurrilous, often foul mouthed, but always funny. From early examples like 'We are Fred Karno's army' to the rather earthier 'I don't want to be a soldier' they catch perfectly the attitude of the ordinary soldier, powerless in a conflict he can do little about:

> I don't want to be a soldier,
> I don't want to go to War.
> I'd rather hang around
> Piccadilly Underground
> Living on the earnings of a high born lady. 35

Funny, yes, but tinged with more than a degree of regret. And, of course, there is also the soldier's less than accepting attitude towards those who are not sharing the discomforts of his trench alongside him.

The ability to laugh at misfortune is what makes the soldier's songs interesting and takes them out of the realms of mindless rounds or repetition designed to keep the mind occupied when discomfort or even death are close at hand. Sometimes there is even a degree of utter glee in considering what might lie ahead:

> Hush! Here comes a whiz-bang
> And it's making straight for you:
> And you'll see all the wonders of No Man's Land
> If a whiz-bang gets you. 36

A humorous postcard from 1917.

Often the soldiers' songs of the Great War take an irreligious look at what is happening. Often the songs are parodies of hymns, tunes that the men all knew but with words that were rather different. 'When this Bloody War is Over', for example, sung to the tune of 'What a Friend We Have in Jesus' or 'Wash Me in the Water' which was sung to the melody of 'Wash Me in the Blood of the Lamb'. Or this one, sung to the tune of 'Oh God, our Help in Ages past':

> John Wesley had a little dog,
> He was so very thin.
> He took him to the gates of Hell
> And threw the bastard in. [37]

The words have no relevance to the predicament of the men in their trenches but the bitterness and rancour are there for all to see.

Humorous poetry was another way of laughing at adversity. Such verse was a million light years away from the noble sacrifice of Rupert Brooke but it certainly made its point. Much of it was published in *The Wipers Times*, the trench newspaper founded in February 1916 and published by Lt-Col. F. J. Roberts until the end of the war. The paper's content was highly satirical and was fertile ground for men who were willing to laugh at themselves as well as the General Staff and those in command:

> Take a wilderness of ruin
> Spread with mud quite six feet deep;
> In this mud cut channels,
> Then you have the line we keep.
>
> Get a lot of Huns and plant them
> In a ditch across the way;
> Now you have war in the making,
> As waged here from day to day.
> (Anon) [38]

Humour, at least, was safe. It stopped men thinking too deeply about what faced them. Even Paul von Hindenburg was moved to comment, 'I read no poetry now, it might soften me.' And it was not just in France that humour surfaced to help men cope with the strain of incessant war and bloodshed. Exotic experience was one thing; sand and flies were something else:

> There's sand and sand for miles around,
> It clogs yer mouf and eyes;
> And when yer aint a chewin' sand
> Yer chewin' bags o' flies.
>
> Blokes say this place aint arf so bad,
> Some say yer cannot beat it;

I like old Egypt a bit myself
But, blimey, not enough to eat it.
(Anon) 39

The Great War saw a proliferation of humorous postcards. Often these cards were drawn by men who had never been within fifty miles of the front. But when they were the work of artists like Fred Mackain and Bruce Bairnsfather (a serving soldier) they were resonant with reality and were clearly pieces of humorous art with which the soldiers could identify. I've been there, I've done that, they could say and happily send the card to their loved ones when they knew that the censor would quickly pounce on them if they had tried to say, in words, anything remotely similar.

Mackain's 'Sketches of Tommy's Life' were comic postcards but his drawings were amazingly accurate, from the puttees around the men's legs to the long service stripes on their arms. Bairnsfather's Old Bill, a character straight out of the Old Contemptibles, seemed to catch the mood of the moment and appeared many times on postcards and in booklets like *Fragments from France*.

The British Tommy was a sentimental soul and loved nothing more than to buy and send home silk postcards that had been produced – almost as a form of cottage industry – by the women of France and Belgium. But the humorous cards of Mackain and Bairnsfather certainly ran them close, hugely popular and with enough relevance to make everyone, soldiers and their families, stop and think for a few minutes.

Sketches of Tommy's life Up the line — N° 4 The only time I ever saw a man cry was when one of our chaps dropped his rifle in the mud after spending exactly two hours cleaning it.

The postcards of F. Mackain were accurate and funny. They were much loved by British soldiers who saw them as a true picture of their lives in France.

The Dover Patrol

The Dover Patrol was one of the great British success stories of the war. Established in 1914, it was intended to provide cover and defence for the Straits of Dover and deny the Germans access to the English Channel. Across the Dover Straits men of the BEF would travel, replacements or leave men, the wounded and those going to the front for the first time. So it was an essential part of the war effort.

The Dover Patrol force consisted of destroyers, mine sweepers, trawlers and monitors. There were also aeroplanes and airships. And at night the Straits were illuminated by flares and lights as a way of preventing U Boats slipping through on the surface. Mines and anti-submarine nets added to the defences.

Numerous small ship actions between British and German destroyers occurred on a fairly regular basis. Perhaps the most famous took place on 20 April 1917 near to the Goodwin Sands. Two British destroyers, the *Broke* and *Swift*, came across seven German ships and, despite being heavily outnumbered, immediately engaged them.

One German destroyer was sunk by torpedo and the *Broke*, under the command of Teddy Evans – a man who had accompanied Robert Falcon Scott to the Antarctic on his last expedition – rammed another. The two ships clung together and close quarter fighting with pistol and cutlass took place before the German destroyer slipped away and sank. The *Broke* was towed back to Dover in triumph.

The Dover Patrol, using their heavy gunned monitors, bombarded the Belgian coat on many occasions and on St George's Day 1918 launched an assault on the submarine bases at Zeebrugge and Ostend. The attacks were costly, three obsolete cruisers filled with cement being used to block the canal and thus bottle up German U Boats in their bases, but they were successful. Eight Victoria Crosses were won during the action.

Mesopotamia and Palestine

Despite the disaster at Kut, by the end of 1916 the campaign in Mesopotamia was progressing reasonably satisfactorily. The plan was, after the Turks had been expelled, for Mesopotamia to become independent state under a British mandate and thus ensure, for the foreseeable future, the oil wells of the region. Progress was slow, however, as the Turks were proving a dogged and determined foe.

The lesson of Kut had been well learned and Britain was certainly not going to make the same mistake again. By the end of the war there were nearly 600,000 British soldiers serving in Mesopotamia, enduring the sun, sand and flies that were every bit as bad as the plagues in the Old Testament.

They were also fighting pitched battles like the one at Sannaiyat where the Ghurkhas blood-lust saw them massacre a Turkish unit – two hundred Turkish bodies were found within a radius of a few hundred yards.

The original aim of the Palestine Campaign was to defend and protect the Suez Canal. An earlier Turkish assault in 1915 had been repulsed and, after the withdrawal from Gallipoli, the area was heavily strengthened with British and Commonwealth troops. Another Turkish attack had taken place in the summer of 1916 but it had been

Above left: Bruce Bairnsfather is perhaps the best known of all British humorous artists. He was a serving soldier rather than a War Artist and his representations of soldiers, Old Bill, in particular, struck a chord with the soldiers at the front.

Above right: A torpedo boat in action in the North Sea.

The Dover Patrol became famous for its exploits in the Dover Straits and in the North Sea. This painting shows a typical destroyer action, something with which all members of the Dover Patrol would have been familiar.

Above left: Ammunition for the guns, shells being brought up to the front in one of the campaigns in the Middle East.

Above right: Lawrence of Arabia, an enigmatic and mysterious figure who played a vital role in the campaign in the Middle East.

Above left: The campaign in Mesopotamia was also grinding remorselessly on. The Turks were a fierce enemy and there were times when the war in the Middle East seemed a long way from a successful conclusion.

Above right: A Christmas card from Baghdad where, as 1917 drew to a close, soldiers were still fighting desperately.

easily beaten back. In the wake of this victory it was decided that Palestine should, like Mesopotamia, also be taken from the Ottoman Empire and Britain, rather than sitting and defending the Canal, went on the offensive.

At this moment a charismatic and mysterious individual appeared on the scene – T. E. Lawrence or, as he is better known, Lawrence of Arabia. Much has been written about Lawrence, most of it pure fiction. The real man was practical and hard headed and knew that if the Arab nations could be brought onto Britain's side there would be far more chance of a successful outcome to the war in the Middle East. At Lawrence's bidding huge sums of money were paid to the Arab leaders and they were almost certainly led to believe, perhaps by Lawrence, perhaps by High Command, that once the Turks were expelled Arab independence would be guaranteed.

However, on 2 November 1917, the Balfour Declaration promised Jews from all over the world a home in Palestine. The motive was clearly financial as Jewish investors and industrialists on both sides of the Atlantic needed to be kept happy. At the end of the nineteenth century the Zionist Movement had actually settled 100,000 Jewish farmers and speculators in the area and the Arabs had made no protest. This, however, was different; this agreement promised a homeland for Jews in a land that the Arabs had always considered theirs by right. It meant that in years to come, when Britain ruled the region by yet another Mandate, there would undoubtedly be serious trouble from both sides.

Now, however, Lawrence began a guerrilla war that saw him and his Arab helpers blow up railway tracks, buildings and bridges behind Turkish lines. He captured Aqaba and kept hundreds of Turkish soldiers engaged in defending strategic positions. Nobody knew where Lawrence and his men would appear next.

Meanwhile, the Egypt Expeditionary Force built a railway line across the Sinai Desert and prepared to move on Jerusalem. The first stage in the campaign, as everybody knew, was the capture of Gaza. Two attempts to take it were made in early 1917 but both resulted in failure and in 6,500 British and Commonwealth casualties. Then the British General Archibald Murray was replaced by Sir Edmund Allenby, a career soldier who had successfully commanded Third Army at the Battle of Arras. He was an impressive man, nicknamed The Bull, and even the Australian and New Zealand soldiers quickly fell under his spell.

Allenby immediately reversed previous thinking and made Beersheba the first objective, rather than Gaza. An elaborate deception campaign was put in place, convincing the Turks that Gaza was the main objective with a smaller attack also being made on Beersheba. On 31 October 1917, cavalry and infantry mounted a lightning assault on Beersheba and occupied the town before the Turks knew what was happening. At the same time an assault was launched on Gaza and Allenby's third force drove a wedge between the two towns, effectively splitting and dividing the Turkish forces.

The key to the campaign was the Australian cavalry. Given their head, these men roamed the desert, charging into the Turks wherever and whenever they found them. Towards the end of December, Allenby's troops closed on Jerusalem and on the seventeenth of the month the city surrendered. Allenby walked calmly and respectfully into the town, the first time the Holy City had been in Christian hands for six hundred years.

1918 – The Final Year

War on the Home Front

As 1918 dawned there remained a serious shortage of food in the shops. The U Boats were still not totally beaten – approximately 300,000 tons of Allied shipping being sunk every month – and in February, rationing of meat, sugar and butter was introduced. This was only partly an economic and supply issue; the introduction of rationing was also intended to curtail the activities of war profiteers. The other thing it did, of course, was to end the hated habit of fighting at the shop doorway for whatever food was available. Now everyone would receive their fair share. They might have to queue and wait but they would get no less – or more – than the woman in front.

Proving that humour was not just the preserve of the man at the front, housewives also developed the ability to laugh at deprivation, as this poem from February 1918 clearly shows:

> O margarine, oh margarine,
> Thy absence causes many a scene.
> I stand in queues mid snow and rain
> To get some more of Thee again.
> Fed up with jam and bloater paste,
> Oh margo, come to me in haste.
> (Anon) [40]

By now the war had been raging for nearly four years and it sometimes seemed as if it would never end. Casualty lists from France remained high and the work in the factories was more demanding than ever. More and more shells were required and while the women munitions workers were undoubtedly earning good money there were times when they wondered if it was all worth it. The attitude of some of their male colleagues was aggressive. They could not quite get it out of their minds that an effective force of women workers might just mean more unemployment after the war.

And, of course, the work itself was both debilitating and dangerous. An explosion at a munitions factory in East London in 1917 had killed several women and destroyed all the nearby houses. There were several more explosions, of lesser or greater degree, throughout the war as faulty workmanship or poor materials caused serious detonations. Even if there was no explosion women would often suffer from ailments like coughs and convulsions and the story of the 'canaries', women whose skin and hair had been turned bright yellow by the chemicals used, is now famous.

THE END OF A PERFECT DAY.

Above left: Rationing was introduced early in 1918. There had been shortages for months, now the government was doing something about it.

Above right: A humorous look at a far from funny situation.

Women munitions workers fulfilled a vital role but their male colleagues did not always approve or help them.

DOING THEIR BIT
A Gardener and a Baker of the
Women's Auxiliary Army Corps

Women of the Land Army.

The introduction of crèches was a major step forward. These began in small factories but were soon introduced in most of the major munitions centres. Now, perhaps for the first time, married women with young children could be sure that their babies were being well looked after while they worked their shift.

The moral welfare of the women was a constant problem for authorities. When thousands of young women were thrown together, for work and leisure, there was a genuine need for help and protection – and, of course, a desire to ensure that they would appear in work the next day. Alcohol abuse was a major problem. In Carlisle, close to the largest munitions factory in the country, the government even went so far as to buy up the local pubs and breweries in the town so that they could control the amount – and quality – of beer available. The state owned public houses of Carlisle were still running in the 1970s.

It was not just in the factories that women were now employed. The Women's Land Army and Women's Forage Corps had been established by Meriel Talbot and Lady Denman in 1917, the aim being to use women workers in traditional male farming roles in order to help food production. [41] If the women in the factories thought the men treated them badly, then the farmers and farm labourers could certainly teach them a thing or two. They doubted that the women were strong enough and determined enough to take on such heavy and demanding work. While the scheme was not universally successful, the vast majority of the Land Army girls delighted in proving them wrong.

People's Shrines

The concept of War Memorials for ordinary soldiers was almost unknown in Britain before the Great War. A diligent searcher might find one or two commemorative monuments – one in the West Wales town of Carmarthen, which remembers the fallen of the Boer War, is a rarity – but, in the main, such memorials as do exist commemorate officers and the sons of landed gentry.

In the Victorian age the professional rank and file soldier had either enlisted in the army as an alternative to a term in prison or was fleeing an unhappy or even dangerous past. He was paid to put his life at risk so to commemorate him if he was killed was neither expected nor desired.

The fallen of the Great War made people stop and think. These weren't what Wellington once called 'the scum of the earth'; they were ordinary, decent men who had enlisted in order to help their country in time of need. And there was no doubt that the casualty lists in this war were enormous. Very few villages managed to escape without two or three of its young men making the ultimate sacrifice and the misguided concept of the Pals Battalions ensured that the towns in the industrial belts of the country would suffer a terrible toll.

In the wake of battles like the Somme, makeshift shrines began to appear on village greens, on street corners and on the pavements. Not unlike the flowers that are now often found on the site of a fatal accident, these shrines were not officially sanctioned and were just an outpouring of sentiment and emotion. They usually consisted of crosses, mementoes and flowers and, once in place, were added to by other bereaved relatives. [42] The government noticed the popularity of these people's shrines and marked them down as a way of commemorating the fallen once the war was ended.

Many churches began to keep Rolls of Honour. These were simply lists of parishioners who had died, a compilation of sacrifice, and were given a place of honour in the church. In years to come these Rolls of Honour were to be the basis for each town's War Memorial but for now they were incomplete and needed to be added to every week. As 1918 began it was clear that was exactly what would happen as the war in France continued with its old, familiar pattern.

Above left: People's Shrines had been established as early as 1916 and there was a growing determination that all of the dead should be remembered. Many churches began to compile Rolls of Honour, lists of men from the parish who had fallen in the conflict. This photograph shows the Chew Magna Roll of Honour being amended.

Above right: Silk postcards asking people to remember a fallen friend or loved ones became enormously popular in 1918.

Lloyd George and Haig

Despite an outward appearance of harmony, a sham that was carefully nurtured by the press, the relationship between the Prime Minister Lloyd George and Douglas Haig had never been good. Put simply, they disliked each other. Lloyd George believed that Haig's tactics of frontal assault were costing Britain needless casualties and it has been argued that, as a consequence, he deliberately kept Haig short of men and materials – possibly in the hope that he would fail on the Western Front. It is an interesting argument but one that has never really been proved.

Haig, himself no mean dissembler, distrusted the adroit and politically wily Lloyd George. He was right to do so for the Welsh wizard clearly intended to rid himself and the army of its military leader in France. As 1918 dawned, Haig was still beyond his reach, however. It did not stop Lloyd George laying the ground for his attack.

By embroiling him in a debate about the Supreme War Council, Lloyd George skilfully managed to isolate the Chief of the General Staff, General Sir William Robertson, and push him into a corner where his position quickly became untenable. General Henry Wilson, yet another arch intriguer, and a man whose dislike of Hague matched that of Lloyd George himself, replaced him.

Unfortunately for Lloyd George events in France now forestalled him. Once the German assaults of the spring began there was never any real opportunity or likelihood of replacing the man at the top. Even though Lloyd George accompanied the dismissal of Robertson by replacing Lord Derby with Lord Milner as Minister of War – something that was clearly intended as the beginning of a complete clear out – his reforms stalled. Haig continued as Commander-in-Chief and Lloyd George never again managed to find himself in a position where he could even contemplate getting rid of Britain's senior general.

The Ludendorff Offensive

The German Armistice with Russia in November 1917 meant that Ludendorff could now release the huge forces he had been obliged to maintain on the Eastern Front. Fifty-two Divisions were quickly moved to France, ready for what would clearly be a final push for victory. Even with these fifty-two extra Divisions the forces facing each other across No Man's Land were still roughly equal. The advantage Ludendorff had came not in numbers of men but in new tactics.

The plan was deceptively simple. There was to be no preliminary bombardment of several days to warn the enemy or destroy the ground and the attacking troops were moved quietly up to the front at night. Importantly, unlike all previous assaults, this one was not going to involve long lines of men attacking across a broad front. Units of fast moving storm or shock troops would rush forward to capture key points, leaving any pockets of resistance for the second or third wave of attackers to wipe out.

On 21 March 1918, Ludendorff struck. That morning the countryside was blanketed by dense fog and when a short but intense bombardment in the area between Arras and St Quentin decimated the British positions it took everyone by surprise. Gas shells, their poisonous fumes mixing with the fog, added to the chaos. When the shock troops went in, some of them using new flame throwers, they found that, on many parts of the front, trenches and units had been simply obliterated and despite desperate defence the British line began to crumble. Soon they were forced to retreat, falling back forty miles and losing 200,000 casualties – as well as a further 80,000 who had been taken prisoner.

Petain, despite being under attack himself, sent reinforcements. Haig was grateful yet, even then, it was clear that the main concern of the French was to safeguard Paris. Haig, on the other hand, wanted and needed to keep open his lines of communication with the French ports.

Haig, who had always been contemptuous of the idea of Supreme Command, at last began to see the value of a united approach. At a meeting in Doullens on 26 March, with British forces still retreating, General Ferdinand Foch was given supreme command of all Allied armies. It was an appointment that seemed to please everyone, even the American General Pershing who had always insisted that the USA would manage its own destiny and submit to no control but his.

Foch could not direct or command the armies of the Allies as they fought. That was down to individual commanders like Haig and Pershing. But he could control the reserves and he quickly showed himself adept at using such forces. Rather than throw in reserves or extra troops just to shore up a crumbling defence, he kept them back and, when the time was right, used them to counter attack.

The German attack gradually began to lose its impetus about two weeks into the campaign. On 5 April it was halted with both sides exhausted and desperate for a respite. The Germans had inflicted heavy casualties on the enemy but they had also suffered themselves from the stubborn resistance of the British. Low flying aircraft of the RFC – which became the RAF on 1 April – added to their discomfort.

Importantly, as they advanced the Germans had seen the quality and quantity of British equipment and supplies. They had come across French shops and farmhouses where there was no such thing as food shortages. As the advance began to lose its way many of the German soldiers, used to the privations imposed by the British blockade on their homeland, became more interested in plundering the wine and food stores than they were in attacking the enemy.

The Ludendorff Offensive – Phase Two

The respite was short lived. On 9 April, phase two of the Ludendorff Offensive began. This time the attack was in Flanders, on the front between Armentieres and La Bassee and was again preceded by a short but intense artillery bombardment. On the flanks of the attack the Germans met stern resistance from British troops but in the centre it was a very different story. The line here was held by a Portuguese Division, inexperienced and unhappy in what was, for them, a new experience. They broke and ran within minutes of the attack beginning. Despite the gap being plugged by Scottish troops a thirty mile gap had been smashed in the Allied line.

The fear now was that Amiens and Hazebrouck, important railway junctions, might fall. Foch quickly deployed men behind Amiens and Haig threw his last troops into the battle. It was now that he issued his famous order of the day:

When the Ludendorff Offensive was launched in
March 1918 it was a campaign fought with new
tactics – no prolonged artillery bombardment
– and new weapons like the terrible flame thrower.

German soldiers in their dugouts.

Ferdinand Foch, who became Supreme
Commander of the Allied Armies as the
Ludendorff Offensive was still raging.

OUT FOR VICTORY.

TOMMY.
" I want Peace right enough—but I'll finish

By the middle of 1918 the desire for peace was strong in all armies but everyone knew there was no stopping, not now with the war so nearly won.

'With our backs to the wall and believing in the justice of our cause each one must fight to the end ... There is no other course open to us but to fight it out. Every position must be held to the last man.' 43

German troops advanced steadily, taking Passchendaele, the village and ridge that the British had captured with such terrible losses only the year before. Soon even the Ypres salient and the town itself were under serious threat. Four French Divisions were sent to the area between Ypres and the coast to help the Belgians defend their last piece of unoccupied territory and by 29 April the German attack had again run out of steam.

The Ludendorff Offensive – Phase Three

German losses in the 1918 offensives so far had amounted to nearly 350,000 but Ludendorff knew that the decisive moment had come. From this point on it was not a case of continuing the war for another three or four years – victory or defeat for Germany depended on what happened next.

A pause of about a month now occurred as the Germans prepared for a new assault Ludendorff knew that he could not delay for long – the longer he waited, the stronger the Allies became as American troops were now pouring like gold dust into France. Unfortunately for Ludendorff, his soldiers had been, quite literally, ground down by pressure of their own offensives, in precisely the same way that the British and French had been worn down by their repeated offensives of the past four years. But despite this, the Germans still achieved initial success.

Ludendorff's aim this time was to attack the French along the Notre Dame Ridge, an area that was considered quiet and isolated. It was for this reason that Haig and Foch had sent the British IX Corps to the region. They had been severely mauled in the earlier offensives and, for the moment, Haig did not consider them in any condition to act as front line troops. Yet that was exactly what they became when the German assaults began with what was now their usual ferocious but short lived bombardment on 27 May.

Shells and more shells – that was what the armies needed.

American troops putting on their gas masks before an attack.

British soldiers in practise for the final assault.

Fourteen German Divisions quickly broke through the British and French lines, advancing ten miles in a single day. It was the biggest advance since 1914 and within a week German forces had reached the River Marne, just fifty miles from Paris. French losses amounted to nearly 100,000, British to 28,000. Once again, however, German troops were disheartened by the quality of equipment they found, equipment that had been abandoned or discarded by Allied troops as they fled the battlefield. How can we possibly win, they asked themselves, when we are facing material and weapons like this?

It was time, now, to throw in the American units. On 6 June they attacked and retook Belleau Wood. They suffered heavy casualties but the experience gave them confidence and made Ludendorff revise his opinion on the quality and durability of American soldiers.

A week later Ludendorff's troops crossed the Marne but now the French had withdrawn to take up positions on either side of Rheims. From there they were able to shell and machine gun the advancing Germans in what became known as the Second Battle of the Marne. It was Ludendorff's last throw of the dice. Realising the position was untenable, he pulled his forces back over the Marne and decided to go on the defensive until the Allies had been worn down. It never happened.

The Allied Counter Attack

On 24 July, Foch called Haig, Pershing and Petain to a meeting at his headquarters. It was time, he had decided, to go on the offensive. The British would attack in the north, around the Ypres area; the French would advance in the centre; and the Americans would assault the southern sector near the old battleground of Verdun.

On 8 August, the British offensive began. They had learned something from the recent German offensives and this time there was no prolonged bombardment before troops went over the top. In addition, over 450 tanks, heavy Mark Vs and lighter Whippets which had a top speed twice that of the Mark Vs, were used and, to everyone's surprise, an advance of six miles was made before the attack slowed and stalled.

Even this setback proved useful. Previously, all military strategy had insisted attacks should be made against the enemy's strongest points. Now Haig, like Ludendorff before him, discovered that it was easier and less costly to halt an advance when it came up against strong resistance and then probe for weak points in the defence. It was a tactic the Allies would use to the end of the war and it had all begun with that British assault in early August. As if sensing the significance, Ludendorff called 8 August 'the black day of the German Army'.

Over the next week or so, Allied attacks were launched on various parts of the German lines. In the last of them, on 12 September, the Americans overran the St Mihiel salient to the south of Verdun, a success they achieved in just forty-eight hours. Pershing had insisted that the Americans should fight independently and, while earlier American assaults along the line of the Meuse had failed dismally, this time they achieved amazing success. Coordinated air attacks, with low flying fighters under Colonel Billy Mitchell strafing the German troops, was an important part of the American success and was something Allied commanders quickly noted and incorporated into their own offensives.

The Allied attacks were another psychological blow in the coffin of the German Army, utterly destroying the soldier's belief in German invincibility. They would continue to fight but now nobody had any real hope of victory. By 18 September the British First, Third and Fourth Armies stood in front of the Hindenburg Line, the Siegfried Stellung; the very positions they had held before the Ludendorff Offensive began back in March.

At this point the American units, desperate for a more challenging role, were moved to the wooded Argonne area where their enthusiasm eventually helped them overcome the difficult terrain and the dogged resistance of the enemy. It was not easy for them, American forces enduring 100,000 casualties in the fighting, but they persevered. Notable American generals of the Second World War were blooded here, men like Colonel Marshall and the indomitable George Patton.

The Siegfried Stellung was breached by British forces on 5 October and now the German Army, although still fighting bravely, was being pushed back on all fronts. By 1 November the British had reached the Scheldt. It really did seem as if the end might be in sight.

Other Theatres of War

If the summer and early autumn of 1918 saw huge Allied successes in France, there were also further victories in other parts of the world.

At the end of 1917 French President Georges Clemenceau had recalled General Serrail from Salonika and Franchet d'Esperey was left in command. The expeditionary force had been idle for so long that it came as something of a surprise when, on 15 September 1918, d'Esperey decided to attack. It was a major surprise for the Bulgarians, too. Poorly equipped and demoralised, they surrendered immediately. Bulgaria asked for an Armistice and promptly withdrew from the war. With all of southern Europe now open to him d'Esperey advanced almost unopposed and by the time the war ended had actually reached the Danube.

Another front was opened when, on 2 August, an Allied force under General Poole landed at Archangel in Russia. The Allies had, following the assassination of the Czar and all his family at Ekaterinburg in the Ural Mountains, become fearful that the Bolsheviks might seize arms and ammunition that had been given to the Russians earlier in the war.

The expeditionary force, consisting of French, British, American and Polish troops, came courtesy of an invitation from the 'White Russians', supporters of the deposed Czar and the Royalist regime. It was an ill-fated campaign that ran on for a few years and was, inevitably, doomed to failure. Archangel was eventually abandoned and returned to Russian control. It had been a totally pointless affair, as one disgruntled British participant confirmed:

'I remember the cold, more than anything else. I was serving on board a Royal Fleet Auxiliary tanker at the time. We were just frozen in, couldn't get out or do anything. It was so cold that if you touched anything metal you'd pull your skin off when you tried to let go. I don't think we did anything useful. We just sat there.' [44]

Above left: By the middle of 1918 even the makers of humorous postcards could see that the end was not far away.

Above right: A French bomber squadron waits on its aerodrome in the Balkans.

The war in Serbia and the other Balkan states was not just vicious; it was also fought in some of the worst conditions ever encountered by regular soldiers.

That autumn, on the Italian front, General Diaz launched an attack on the town of Vittorio Veneto, effectively splitting the Austro-Hungarian Army in two. The Italians, heavily reinforced by the British Tenth Army, occupied Vittorio Veneto on 29 October and, realising they could not continue the war, the Austro-Hungarians promptly asked for an Armistice. This was duly agreed and signed on 3rd November.

The surrender signalled not just the end of the Austrian Army but also the end of the Austro-Hungarian Empire. In January 1918, when he had published his famous Fourteen Points, President Wilson had already promised that nations like Poland and Czechoslovakia should become independent states – such decisions, he declared, must lie within the remit of the countries themselves, not their previous rulers and certainly not with nations like the USA.

In line with Wilson's promise, within days of the Armistice being signed Hungary had broken away from the old Hapsburg Empire and Czechoslovakia also announced itself an independent republic at exactly the same moment. By becoming 'Allies' one day before the end of the war both countries avoided the war guilt clause of the Treaty of Versailles – Austria herself was not so lucky.

In the Middle East, events were also rapidly moving to a climax. Allenby reached Damascus on 1 October and another Allied army was inching ever closer to the rich oil fields of Mosul. The fighting was still hard and furious but, finally facing assured and utter defeat, Turkey had little alternative but to ask for terms. Turkish forces duly surrendered on 30 October, the treaty being signed on board the battleship HMS *Agamemnon*.

With Constantinople now in Allied hands a British fleet was at last able to steam serenely up the Dardanelles. The Sultan was effectively a prisoner of the Allies and the Ottoman Empire, like the Hapsburgs and Romanovs before it, had come to a sudden and disastrous end.

Above left: A standard soldier's field postcard – literally, just fill in the blanks to let the folks back home know you were well.

Above right: Even the Kaiser could tell that the situation in Germany was serious. The British blockade was strangling the country and people were starving in the streets. Yet he, like the rest of his militaristic regime, fought on, until finally he was told that the soldiers might fight for Germany but they would not fight for him. He abdicated shortly afterwards.

In East Africa the redoubtable von Lettow-Vorbeck continued to harry the British right to the end. His biggest problem continued to be lack of supplies – a Zeppelin had even attempted to relieve his position in November 1917 but had been forced back to Bulgaria without success. A joint British-Portuguese force chased him into Tanganyika and then into Northern Rhodesia. And it was here that he heard the news of the Kaiser's abdication on 9 November. Faced with no alternative, von Lettow-Vorbeck surrendered, undefeated. By this time his army had been reduced to just 1,300 troops but he had effectively kept 200,000 Allied soldiers at bay for several years, a truly significant achievement.

The End of the War Approaches

As early as January 1918 President Woodrow Wilson of the USA had put forward his Fourteen Points. These were a series of suggestions that, Wilson hoped, would prevent anything like the Great War from ever occurring again. They included items like the outlawing of secret treaties, making the oceans of the world free for everyone and self determination for all nations. They also included the creation of a League of Nations which would, hopefully, arbitrate for all countries, big or small.

With defeat staring him in the face Ludendorff now began looking for a way out. He decided that Germany needed to become a democratic nation and, with amazing autocratic arrogance, duly imposed this on the country. Prince Max of Baden, a liberal, was appointed Chancellor and Social Democrats were even pulled into the government. It was, of course, all a sham. Ludendorff and the other generals intended to use Prince Max and even the Fourteen Points merely as a way of stopping hostilities, leaving the German Army unbroken and ready to fight again at some stage in the future.

On 4 October, the Germans asked for an Armistice, sending their request to President Wilson, a man they considered idealistic and even a little weak. Their request included a section that accepted Wilson's Fourteen Points. If Prince Max thought he was deluding Wilson then he was wrong. Wilson replied that any Armistice had to be settled by the relevant military commanders and, most importantly, unrestricted submarine warfare must stop immediately.

When the German leaders met to discuss the situation on 17 October Ludendorff had changed his mind. The Allied offensive, he now thought, was running out of steam and there was virtue in carrying on the fight. Prince Max and the new democratic government dismissed such a view as delusional.

Unrestricted submarine warfare was immediately called off and Wilson's condition that an Armistice had to be settled by the military leaders was fully accepted. And then the haggling began. Whatever world leaders might say in support of the Fourteen Points, they all had their own agendas. Clemenceau desperately wanted the Rhineland for France, as much for a buffer between the two nations as for its economic value. Lloyd George wanted the German fleet, all of it, safely locked up in Scapa Flow or some other British port. Unlike the idealistic Wilson, the idea of a just peace did not appeal to any of the European leaders – they wanted their revenge and the spoils of victory.

As negotiations continued, as politicians debated and argued, the war carried on and men continued to die. The Allied Armies moved steadily forward, progress being

An Armistice was signed in the Forest of Compiegne on 11 November 1918 and all fighting stopped at 11.00 a.m. that morning.

Above left: Allied representatives at the signing of the Armistice, outside the railway carriage that was used for the occasion.

Above right: Immediate rejoicing broke out all over Europe. In London there were wild scenes of drunkenness and debauchery. It was understandable; the Armistice had brought to an end four years of unmitigated horror.

held up by stubborn German resistance. They knew that conditions in Germany were desperate, and knew that the British blockade had inflicted serious food shortages on German civilians. They knew that they were winning the war but it was anybody's guess as to when the conflict might finish.

Peace at Last

On 26 October, Kaiser Wilhelm unexpectedly dismissed Ludendorff and left Berlin bound for Army Headquarters at Spa. The position was clearly desperate and when Austria-Hungary pulled out of the war in early November it left Germany's soft underbelly cruelly exposed. Immediately, Allied commanders began to lay plans for an attack into the southern part of the country.

German naval leaders now decided that it was time to pitch the High Seas Fleet, for one last time, against the might of the Royal Navy. It was to be a death or glory affair that could only ever end one way and the sailors simply refused to sail. They had no desire to die at this late stage of the war and so, on 29 October, they mutinied. The town and port of Kiel were soon in their hands and Prince Max and the new democratic government in Berlin saw shades of the Russian Revolution swarming towards them. There was now no alternative but to seek a peace agreement before revolution overwhelmed everything.

Matthias Erzberger, a leading Jewish politician of the Centre Party – his Jewish background and political stance being an important factor in the later rise of the Nazi Party – was appointed to head the German Armistice Commission. On 7 November, he requested a meeting with Foch and later that night, long after darkness had fallen, he crossed the frontier. At 8.00 a.m. the following morning, Erzberger and the other delegates met with General Foch and Admiral Wemyss in a railway carriage in the forest of Compiegne. Foch read out the terms by which the Allies would agree to a cease fire. They were harsh but with revolution now exploding across the country they could hardly be refused. Nevertheless, Erzberger asked for time to consider and passed on the terms and conditions to Berlin.

By now the revolutionaries had taken to the streets of Berlin and a republic was proclaimed. Prince Max handed over control to Ebert, leader of the Social Democratic party, and at Military Headquarters the news was broken to the Kaiser. He was told, quite clearly, that while the soldiers might well continue to fight for Germany they would no longer fight for an Emperor. Kaiser Wilhelm immediately went into exile in Holland and two days later formally signed his abdication. He never saw or returned to Germany again.

The new republican government quickly ordered Erzberger to sign the Armistice agreement. There was no other way of avoiding revolution. The agreement was signed at 5.00 a.m. on 11 November and fighting along the Western Front ceased at 11.00 a.m. that morning. In the forest of Compiegne, Foch nodded briefly to Erzberger and left the carriage without shaking hands. The war was finally over.

The Aftermath

Occupation and Defeat

With Germany defeated, her troops immediately laid down their arms. Allied forces promptly moved up to the left bank of the Rhine and took control of three strategic bridgeheads. A significant detachment of British troops was based at Cologne; the French at Mainz and the Americans in Coblenz provided similar garrisons. These were occupying troops, land for fifty miles beyond each bridgehead coming under Allied control.

A large number of U Boats had been scuttled by their crews as the war ended but those that remained afloat were soon in British hands. On 21 November, the German High Seas Fleet, consisting of eleven battleships, five battle cruisers and numerous smaller craft, also surrendered, sailing into Scapa Flow behind the light cruiser *Cardiff*. Having obtained the fleet, nobody in the British government or Admiralty really knew what to do with the ships and they lay rusting at their moorings for the next seven months.

With their crews still on board, it was inevitable that something had to happen. In June 1919, the *Friedrich der Grosse*, flagship at the Battle of Jutland, suddenly hoisted her battle ensigns, a signal that was immediately picked up by the other captive ships:

'German flags rose to the mastheads of over seventy vessels – and then they began to sink. The "Frederich der Grosse," the "Konig," the "Von der Tann," battleships and battle cruisers that had been the pride of the Kriegsmarine, slowly settled at their moorings and disappeared beneath the waves.' 45

The German sailors had scuttled their ships rather than leave them in captivity, a gesture of defiance that exasperated and annoyed the British but which, really, had little overall effect.

Germany's air force had been disbanded almost immediately the Armistice was signed, the planes broken up or scrapped. It was the same with weapons like tanks, machine guns and artillery pieces. The very machines of war were being taken away from Germany and there was not, as yet, even a Peace Treaty in place.

A total of 8,538,315 men had been killed in the conflict; another 21,219,452 had been wounded or injured. Over five million Britons had taken part in the war, nearly 800,000 of them being killed. Twelve million tons of shipping, Allied and neutral, had gone to the bottom of the ocean and, in the wake of the war, Spanish flu was ravaging the world – some people say that more died from flu than were killed in the war. There was huge resentment towards Germany, many believing that they and they alone were

On 21 November, the German High Seas Fleet surrendered to Britain, sailing behind the cruiser *Cardiff* into the anchorage of the Grand Fleet in Scapa Flow.

Now that they had the High Seas Fleet the British government did not seem to know what to do with it. In the end the German sailors took matters into their own hands and scuttled their ships before the startled British could do anything about it.

The last German battleship goes down in Scapa Flow.

responsible for the carnage. Small wonder that Clemenceau, the President of France, was to comment, 'We must squeeze Germany like an orange, until the pips squeak.'

Old Empires had disintegrated under the pressure of war, the Hapsburg, Romanov and Ottoman dynasties simply disappearing in the latter stages of the conflict. The beginnings of new power bases, the USSR in particular, were seen for the first time and the USA confirmed itself as the most powerful nation in the world. The British Empire had bankrupted itself and was already dead in the water, even though it did not realise it and struggled on for another fifty years. Truly, the Great War was the most significant event the world had ever seen.

The Treaty of Versailles

As yet, however, there was no treaty in place to bring an official end to hostilities, just a temporary Armistice. The Paris Peace Conference began its work at Versailles on 18 January 1919. The four main participants were Lloyd George of Britain, Clemenceau of France, America's President Wilson and Orlando of Italy.

Significantly, there was no German or Austrian involvement at Versailles. Instead, German delegates were arbitrarily summoned to Versailles on 7 May and told the terms they were now expected to sign. Failure to do so would result in a resumption of the war. Germany was exhausted, her army and navy already destroyed. She had no alternative and in the famous Hall of Mirrors, the very place where the German Empire had been declared in 1871, her delegates signed the Treaty.

The peace terms were harsh, clearly designed to make Germany suffer and pay for the war. The mood at Versailles had been bitter all along, the Allied nations seeming to be greedy for revenge and Clause 231 forcing Germany to accept full blame for the conflict, was a particularly bitter pill for them to swallow. The reparations or war damage money they had to pay – amounting to billions of pounds – effectively ruined the German economy for years to come.

Alsace Lorraine, seized by Germany after the Franco-Prussian War, was returned to France while German territory and land on the west bank of the Rhine was to be

A British armoured car in the streets of Cologne. It was an Allied occupation that left nobody, not even the British who just wanted to go home, particularly happy.

occupied by Allied forces for the next fifteen years. This, Clemenceau believed, would provide an effective buffer between France and Germany. It also denied Germany the great industrial wealth of the Saar Basin and the Ruhr coalfield, areas that had been instrumental in her economic growth and strength during the latter years of the nineteenth and early part of the twentieth centuries.

Germany was also to lose all her colonies which promptly became mandates under British and French control. Her army was reduced to just 100,000 men and she was allowed no air force at all. Her navy was severely limited, her fleet having already been impounded and the number of sailors she was allowed was restricted to 15,000. She was to own and operate no submarines of any sort.

The Treaty of Versailles was a vindictive and, ultimately, self destructive piece of legislation. With hindsight it is easy to see the resentment it caused in Germany and in the minds of most Germans. You do not have to look too far to see that the origins of Adolph Hitler's rise to power and, ultimately, of the Second World War, lie within its clauses. Yet in 1919 people were still too subjective to make clear and careful judgements about how the Great War should be finally laid to rest.

Ultimately, five treaties were drawn up between 1919 and 1920, one for each of the defeated nations – Germany, Austria, Hungary, Bulgaria and Turkey. Between them they changed the map of Europe and created new countries like Czechoslovakia, Estonia, Latvia and Lithuania. Poland, an ancient kingdom that had been swallowed up by Russia and Germany many years before, was recreated and given a strip of land taken from Germany, the Polish Corridor, to allow it access to the sea. Hitler's quest to reclaim the Polish Corridor was, like Gavrilo Princip's shooting of Franz Ferdinand, the spark that ignited a worldwide war.

In the Middle East, following the demise of Turkey, the mandates and promises in regions such as Palestine, Iraq and Syria stored up a legion of problems that would unravel and cause havoc in the final years of the twentieth century. But, for the moment, peace had come and the future could look after itself.

Donkeys or Lions?

Ludendorff once said that the British fought like lions – a colleague promptly responded, 'But they are lions led by donkeys.' It is hard to get that image out of your mind. It's one that has been reinforced by films and books across the years. But is it actually true?

The generals who went to war in 1914 had never seen anything like this before. They were, in the main, cavalry men and their experience of combat was based on colonial skirmishes and the campaigns against the Boer guerrillas. The Great War was a static war, one where defence invariably dominated and if the generals did have one serious flaw it was in their inability to learn lessons from hard experience.

Common military thinking at the time said that the most effective form of attack should be launched against the enemy's strongest point. And so, until the advances of 1918, that's exactly what the generals did – they threw their men against the strongest parts of the German lines, time after time after time. That is what is so unforgivable.

Above left: The signing of the Treaty of Versailles in the Hall of Mirrors, 28 June 1919. British officers stand on tables and chairs to get a glimpse of the historic occasion.

Above right: With peace came the chance to sit and grieve for lost loved ones. This romantic Welsh language postcard laments the death of the poet Hedd Wyn who was killed six weeks before winning his bardic chair at the 1917 Eisteddfod.

Only in 1918 did the message finally sink in – attack the weak spots, leave the strongholds for later.

Revisionist historians now claim that in 1918 Haig won the greatest victory ever achieved by British force of arms. Maybe so, but he also oversaw some of the worst disasters of the war. He was always looking for the chance to unleash his waiting cavalry and could not understand the concept of minimal gains. If he did finally learn his lesson in time to achieve a remarkable victory in those final hundred days, it certainly took him a long time to get there. It was a victory achieved with the blood and sacrifice of his men.

And yet it is hard to know what else Haig could have done. When fluid or open war was fought it could be dramatically effective, as Allenby showed in Palestine. When Allenby commanded a Battalion in France, however, he was as helpless as everyone else.

Interestingly, very little criticism of Haig was ever delivered by his own men. Criticism has come from historians but not from the men of the British Army. It was as if they could see or sense the problems with which he was struggling. And so there is no real answer to the question, donkeys or lions? A little bit of both, perhaps?

The Great Clear Up

In the wake of the Armistice and Treaty of Versailles the killing fields of Flanders and France began to return to normal. Within a few years the trench systems were ploughed over and returned to their pre-war state – even though farmers still dig up, and sometimes die from, unexploded shells every year.

Above left: The lasting image of the Great War – 'In Flanders Fields the poppies blow/ Between the crosses, row on row.'

Above right: Almost there. British guns at Cologne celebrate the signing of the Treaty of Versailles – British troops know it won't be long before they can head for home.

It was not long before trips were being operated to the battlefields – war tourism had arrived. Many of the early visitors were people who had lost friends or relatives in the conflict – in the early days, at least, few soldiers made the return journey. They had seen enough of the battlefields to last them a hundred years.

The Imperial (soon to be renamed Commonwealth) War Graves Commission began its work, huge cemeteries being created across northern France. The bodies of soldiers, buried out of necessity on the battlefield, were exhumed and reburied in these simple but evocative graveyards that are, even now, visited by thousands every year.

In 1920, it was agreed that the body of an unidentified soldier should be brought from France and buried in Westminster Abbey. The date for the ceremony was 11 November 1920. The Unknown Soldier symbolised the thousands of men who had died in the war, particularly those who had no known grave, and touched the heart of all the people of Britain.

The Cenotaph in Whitehall, designed by the renowned architect Sir Edwin Lutyens, was unveiled at the same time. It was never intended to be a permanent monument, the original being made out of wood and board, but the popularity of the people's shrines and the demand for permanent monuments to the fallen caused a radical change of mind. The Cenotaph, created out of Portland stone, is now the centre of the Armistice Day parade and celebration every November.

Virtually every community in Britain demanded and got its own war memorial. It has been estimated that there are over 35,000 memorials in the country, most of them bearing Kipling's choice of words – 'Their name liveth for ever more.'

All over Britain, towns and cities celebrated peace and the return of their soldiers with Victory Day parades. Sometimes these parades were delayed and did not take place until two years after the war ended. The original plans for demobilisation divided men into groups, those who had jobs to go to being discharged first. This

The last meal in Cologne. British soldiers are heading for home.

War tourism begins. Men and women examine a battered and broken British tank. The soldiers have gone, only the memories remain.

The aftermath. The true cost of the war was about to be revealed.

Peace Day celebrations in one of many British towns.

The Cenotaph is ready, 11 November 1920.

Simple crosses but a world of meaning.

Victory celebrations in Pembroke Dock, summer of 1920.

The Thiepval Memorial on the Somme, designed by Lutyens, standing as a memorial to the thousands of men who have no known grave.

often led to a situation where the last men in were the first men out and was clearly unfair. The government tried hard to facilitate the release of time-served men but, with Germany still occupied, demob took time. By February 1920 there were still 125,000 'hostilities only' soldiers waiting to go home. Small wonder, then, that some of the victory celebrations were delayed.

For many, however, there could be no coming home. For many there was not even a known grave. These were men who had just disappeared, perhaps blown to pieces by shells or perhaps drowned in the mud of Passchendaele. They were commemorated on the memorials at Thiepval on the Somme and on the Menin Gate in Ypres. The two memorials remain a hugely powerful and significant statement to man's inhumanity to man. And their greatest tragedy is that they have not stopped war recurring, time after time. The belief that this, the Great War, was the war to end all wars has been proven to be an utter fallacy.

And what about the idea that all the soldiers would come home to a better world? As they would soon discover, that too was a fallacy, a dream that had flourished and then died as surely as if they had been swallowed by the mud of Passchendaele. But then, as the man once said, that is another story.

The memorial to the Welsh Division at Mametz Wood, lonely, brave and a symbol of suffering for all who fell in the Great War.

Notes

1. David James Smith *One Morning in Sarajevo* (Weidenfeld & Nicolson, London, 2008) p. 82
2. Ibid p. 71
3. Phil Carradice *Penarth: A Town in Conflict* (Penarth Press, Penarth, 2006) P19
4. Andrew Swift *All Roads Lead to France* (Akeman Press, Bath, 2005)
5. Carradice, p. 31
6. *Penarth Times*, 10 September 1914
7. Phil Carradice *People's Poetry of World War One* (Cecil Woolf Publishers, London, 2008) p. 15
8. Phil Carradice Penarth: *A Town in Conflict* p. 24
9. H. M. Le Fleming *Warships of World War One* (Ian Allan, London, undated) p. 13
10. Keith Middlemas *Command the Far Seas* (Hutchinson, London, 1961) pp. 107-110
11. Geoffrey Bennett *Coronel and the Falklands* (Pan, London, 1962) p. 141
12. Phil Carradice *Penarth: A Town in Conflict* p. 36
13. Tony Allen *Christmas Greetings From the Great War* (Privately printed, 2001) p. 4
14. Phil Carradice *Penarth: A Town in Conflict* p. 35
15. Phil Carradice *People's Poetry of World War One* p. 35
16. Quentin Reynolds *They Fought For the Sky* (Pan, London, 1960) p. 57
17. Ibid pp. 28-29
18. Jan Morris *Fisher's Face* (Penguin, London 1996) p. 199
19. K. Cooper and J. E. Davies *Cardiff Pals* (Militaria Cymraeg, Cardiff, 2001) p. 2
20. Conversation with Robert Turnbull Carradice, transcript held by author
21. Jan Morris *Fisher's Face* p. 219
22. Phil Carradice *People's Poetry of World War One* p. 54
23. Martin Middlebrook *The First Day on the Somme* (Penguin, London, 2001)
24. Robert Phillips *The Battle of Mametz Wood, 1916* (CAA, Aberystwyth, 2001) pp. 52-58
25. Donald Macintyre *Jutland* (Pan, London, 1966) p. 112
26. Quentin Reynolds *They Fought For the Sky* p. 154
27. Ibid, pp. 156-157
28. Tony Allen *Christmas Greetings From the Trenches* pp. 28-29
29. Phil Carradice, article in *Picture Postcard Monthly* Nov 2009, p. 26
30. Rupert Brooke *The Complete Poems of Rupert Brooke* (Sidgwick & Jackson, London, 1938)
31. Siegfried Sassoon *War Poems* (Faber, London, 1983)
32. Wilfred Owen *War Poems and Others* (Chatto & Windus, London, 1973)

33. Phil Carradice *People's Poetry of World War One* p. 42
34. Quentin Reynolds *They Fought For the Sky*
35. John and Roger Press *Trench Songs of the First World War* (Cecil Woolf Publishers, London, 2008) p. 11
36. Ibid, p. 30
37. Phil Carradice *People's Poetry of World War One* p. 30
38. Ibid, p. 32
39. Ibid, pp. 38-39
40. *Penarth Times*, 21 February 1918
41. Phil Carradice *Wales At War* (Gomer, Llandysul, 2003) p. 84
42. Neil Oliver *Not Forgotten* (Hodder & Stoughton, London, 2005) pp. 71-72
43. Quoted in *The First World War* (Penguin, London, 1963) p. 223
44. Conversation with Robert Turnbull Carradice, transcript held by author
45. Phil Carradice and Terry Breverton *Welsh Sailors of the Second World War* (Glyndwr Publishing, Cowbridge, 2007) p. 2

Bibliography

Primary Sources

Newspapers and Magazines:

The Bath Chronicle
Fragments from France
More Fragments from France
The Penarth Times
The Penarth Times War Supplement
Picture Postcard Monthly
Punch
The Western Mail
The Wipers Times

Interview:

Robert Turnbull Carradice, October 1964 (held by author)

Secondary Sources

Tony Allen *Christmas Greetings from the Great War* (privately printed, 2001)
Bruce Bairnsfather *Bullets and Billets* (Grant Richards Ltd, London, 1916)
Ian Beckett *Home Front, 1914-1918* (National Archives, London, 2006)
Geoffrey Bennett *Naval Battles of the First World War* (Pan, London, 1974)
Rupert Brooke *The Complete Poems* (Sidgwick & Jackson, London, 1935)
Phil Carradice *A Town in Conflict* (Penarth Press, Penarth, 2006)
   People's Poetry of World War One (Cecil Woolf, London, 2008)
   Wales at War (Gomer, Llandysul, 2003)
Phil Carradice and Terry Breverton *Welsh Sailors of the Second World War*
(Glyndwr Publishing, Cowbridge, 2007)
Alan Clark *The Donkeys* (Mayflower, London, 1961)
K. Cooper and J. E. Davies *The Cardiff Pals* (Militaria Cymraeg, Cardiff, 2001)
Paul Fussell *The Great War and Modern Memory* (OUP, London, 1975)
Peter Hart *Aces Falling* (Weidenfeld & Nicolson, London, 2007)
Ian Hay *The First Hundred Thousand* (Blackwood, London, undated)
Richard Holmes *Tommy* (Harper Collins, London, 2004)

John Laffin *World War I in Postcards* (Alan Sutton, Gloucester, 1988)

Alan Llwyd *Out of the Fire of Hell* (Gomer, Llandysul, 2009)

John Lloyd *Aircraft of World War One* (Ian Allan, London, 1958)

Lyn Macdonald *1914 – 1918* (Penguin, London, 1991)

Donald Macintyre *Jutland* (Pan, London, 1966)

Martin Middlebrook *The First Day on the Somme* (Penguin, London, 2001)

Keith Middlemas *Command the Far Seas* (Hutchinson, London, 1961)

Jan Morris *Fisher's Face* (Penguin, London, 1996)

Neil Oliver *Not Forgotten* (Hodder & Stoughton, London, 2005)

Wilfred Owen *War Poems and Others* (Chatto & Windus, London, 1973)

Robert Phillips *The Battle of Mametz Wood* (CAA, Aberystwyth, 2001)

E. Alexander Powell *Fighting in Flanders* (Heinemann, London, 1914)

John & Roger Press (Editors) *Trench Songs of the First World War* (Cecil Woolf, London, 2008)

Quentin Reynolds *They Fought For the Sky* (Pan, London, 1960)

Siegfried Sassoon *The War Poems* (Faber & Faber, London, 1983)

David James Smith *One Morning in Sarajevo* (Weidenfeld & Nicolson, London, 2008)

Andrew Swift *All Roads Lead to France* (Akeman Press, Bath, 2005)

Alan Wakefield *Christmas in the Trenches* (Sutton, Stroud, 2006)